FEARLESS on the EDGE

by Sarah Bowling

FEARLESS on the EDGE

by Sarah Bowling

ISBN # 1-56441-047-1

Thanks to **Jeanne Halsey** for helping with this manuscript.

Marilyn Hickey Ministries
P.O. Box 17340
Denver, Colorado 80217
United States of America

1-303-770-0400

www.mhmin.org

TABLE OF CONTENTS

INTRODUCTION

And we know that all things work together for good to those who love God,... (Romans 8:28 NKJ).

As a small child, I loved to go to the amusement park in the summer and ride the roller coaster. It was awesome! Up-and-down, around-and-around, back to the loading station...essentially just like LIFE!

We will always have ups-and-downs, we will always have highs-and-lows—*even as Christians*. No one is spared the roller coaster ride called "life," but the key to successfully negotiating its twists-and-turns—fearlessly—lies in knowing what to do in the face of every challenge...and that's what this book is all about.

How do *you* handle life when the ride puts you on the "edge"? In this book you'll discover how to...

- Uncover hidden benefits when your life takes a left turn instead of going "right"

- Turn problems into possibilities, dreadful defeats into miracle moments, and terrifying challenges into life-changing opportunities
- Mold life's mud into stepping stones to satisfaction
- Leap fearlessly off the edge to your miraculous, God-given destiny.

Perhaps you feel like you've lived your entire life on the edge. You can identify with Moses who lived 40 years in the desert—eating sand and tending dimwitted, smelly sheep; or with the Israelites—wandering in the wilderness for 40 years; and with the apostle Paul who trained 13 years before he could minister. Maybe, you are impatient to move to the next level—a 13-year-old Jesus, Who wanted to "be about His Father's business" waited 17 years to embark on His mission to save mankind.

Observe what these former *edge-dwellers* accomplished…Moses freed an entire nation from slavery…the Israelites went from being slaves with little, to landowners with much...Paul wrote much of the New Testament and turned his world upside down with the gospel...and Jesus made it possible for the billions born before and since His Crucifixion to become the sons and daughters of God.

Catch this: God is not through with you. He has not forgotten or abandoned you—and neither is He punishing you. God is *preparing you* for an incredible blessing—one too great for you to imagine. (See II Corinthians 2:9,10.)

The Bible truths found in this book have literally changed my life and the lives of many others. They can change yours, too! As you turn the page and step with me to the brink of your tomorrow—discover how to live "fearless (and victorious) on the edge."

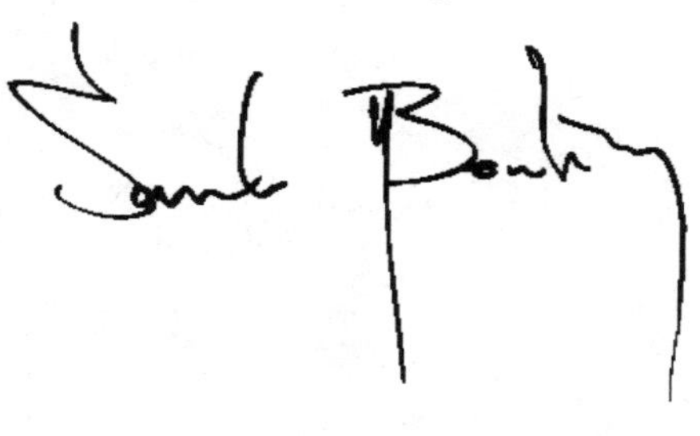

PART ONE
Going *Left* to Go *Right*

Chapter 1
Go "*Right*" to the Edge

Trends come and go, but everybody we know wants to have the *right* car, the *right* husband, the *right* wife, the *right* job, live in the *right* house, and have life be just *right*. Nobody likes the *left*. Nobody wants to get the wrong husband, the wrong wife, or to get *left* out. Most of all, nobody wants to be *left* behind.

Nobody likes the *left*—the place where we feel uncomfortable, disconnected, disjointed, or when things just aren't going smoothly—we all love the *right*. We want to be comfortable on the *right*, this is where we want to live. But interestingly enough, life is a combination of both *left* and *right*. First, I'm going to ask you to reflect on the past year.

Go back to the beginning of this

year, and reflect on what has happened to you. Think about the times you've had *right*. Maybe you had *right* times with your health. Maybe you've lost fifty pounds—and you're thinking, "I'm on the *right* with my health!" That's excellent! Maybe you've had some *right* times with your kids. Some people have kids who have come back to Christ—and we say, "I was *left*, but now I'm on the *right*!"

Seasons of *Rights* and *Lefts*

Have you had some times this year that have not been comfortable, when you've said, "It's not supposed to be this way!"? I would challenge you: those would be your *left* times. "My kids aren't supposed to do that"..."My job is not supposed to be like this"..."My husband is not supposed to be like this"..."My wife is supposed to be something different. She's supposed to have dinner ready for me when I come home." Can you relate to these things?

Here's the situation: our lives are a combination of *lefts* and *rights*. We have seasons in our lives that are *left* and we have seasons that are *right*. Some of us presently are living in a season on the *right* and we're saying, "God, please let it keep going on the *right*, because I hate the *left*."

Even the best athletes have "slumps"; the best marriages have ups and downs; the best generals have fought losing battles. Ecclesiastes 3:1,11 reminds us of this truth, so that we don't let the seasons of our lives catch us off-guard:

> *To everything there is a season, a time for every purpose under heaven:...He has made everything beautiful in its time...except that no one can find out the work that God does from beginning to end* (Ecclesiastes 3:1,11 NKJ).

None of us can see the "big picture" all the time—but all of us can look to our "big" God Who not only sees it, but holds it in the palm of His hand!

Your Worst Day

What was the worst day of *your* life? All of us have bad days, weeks, months, and even years. There are times when it seems like nothing goes *right*—our life has skidded out of control and taken a definite turn to the *left*.

My mother, Marilyn Hickey, tells the story about a time when her life turned *left*:

"Many years ago, Pat Boone came to our church for a special meeting, and everything went wrong. The person who introduced Pat took so long that people started walking out...the sound system broke down...during lunch the waitresses' purses were robbed...then a man grabbed the money from the book table...and the staff person chasing him fell and broke his glasses.

"That same day, my husband got sick, and we received a bad report concerning our son.

"You'd think that was enough...but the next day, I arrived at work to discover that I had forgotten a luncheon speaking engagement and it was too late to cancel. As I left for the meeting, my car broke down and I had to drive the church's difficult-to-handle van. When I arrived for the luncheon, I realized that I was two hours early. I found a place to pray and told God that I was too stressed to minister, but He replied 'Maybe you can't, but I can.'

"When I began to speak, I couldn't imagine what else might go wrong. Suddenly, I was interrupted by a loud popping and cracking noise. A woman jumped up and began shouting, 'I can move my neck! I'm healed!' Later, we learned she had been scheduled for surgery the next day because two bones in her neck were fused together, but God had done an incredible miracle during my teaching."

Can you identify with Mom? Don't lose hope. God is with you even during the worst of times, and will—if you let Him—take your *left* situations, use them for His glory and your benefit, and steer you back on the *right* track.

TV Fiascos

I had what I thought was a "fiasco" experience one time when I was on TV. Everyone has "trying" moments—see if you can relate to this one. I was attempting to be professional, look cool, really fit in, and have these really insightful words to say. But when it came my turn on the program, there was this kid who kept running in and out, touching and hitting me, trying to have a conversation with me. I was trying to be professional with the camera, but this little kid was totally ruining my *right* time.

A few years ago, I had a hard, hard year—I was definitely having a *left* year. There were a lot of things that were uncomfortable, awkward. I wasn't satisfied or contented with a lot of things. Sure, I grew and I learned from all those *left* things... but I also made a decision: "I'm not stopping here. I'm not parking here! I'm not going to let my *left* crush me. My *left* is going to push me to greater success!"

If you are in a season of *left*, I challenge you: "Don't give up!"

> ...*Whatever you do,...do it all in the name of the Lord Jesus, giving thanks to God the Father through him* (Colossians 3:17 NIV).

If you're in a season of *right*, I say, "God bless you!" Either way, remember what the apostle Paul said to the church at Philippi:

> *I have learned the secret of being content in any and every*

> *situation,...I can do everything through him who gives me strength* (Philippians 4:12,13 NIV).

If the *right* seems far away, don't despair. There are keys to help you during your *left* seasons. To find those keys, we're going to look at different people in the Bible who, like you, had seasons of *left* and *right*.

Chapter 2
Recklessly Successful

The Bible tells us that Joseph was a very interesting man who had a lot of seasons of *left* and *right* in his life. Go to Genesis chapter 29 through chapter 37, and let's "set the stage."

Joseph's father, Jacob, loved Rachel, but because of Laban's trickery, Jacob was first married to her sister, Leah, and then later to Rachel. Leah had several children: Reuben, Simeon, Levi, Judah, Issachar, and Zebulun. Leah's maidservant, Zilpah, bore children to Jacob also: Gad and Asher. Rachel's maidservant, Bilhah, bore Dan and Naphtali. And finally Rachel bore Joseph and Benjamin (and then she died after giving birth to Benjamin). So you see that Jacob had two wives—only one whom he loved—and two concubines, and from those four women he had twelve sons (and some daughters). But there was one son whom Jacob really favored: Joseph, the firstborn of Rachel, his favored wife.

Joseph was the *right* son to Jacob. "Oh, this is my son! This is my one and only, number one son! Granted, I have other sons over there—but this one is the ultimate!" Talk about favoritism—the multi-colored coat, the honor above others!

> *Now Israel (Jacob) loved Joseph more than all his children, because he was the son of his old age. And he made him a tunic of many colors* (Genesis 37:3).

With his dad, Joseph is definitely living on the *right*; but, with his brothers, Joseph was really on the *left*:

> *But when his brothers saw that their father loved him more than all his brothers, they hated him*

and could not speak peaceably to him (Genesis 37:5).

With his father, Joseph was the epitome of *right*, but with his brothers, he was the walking definition of *left*. Sometimes we seem to be doing everything *right*—we're on the *right* team, the *right* side, everything's *right*, life is good—but sometimes we get shoved *left* and it's self-inflicted. We do it to ourselves.

Now Joseph had a dream, and he told it to his brothers; and they hated him even more (Genesis 37:5).

Joseph actually had two dreams, and he went to his brothers the first time and said, "I had this great dream, and ultimately what it means is you all are going to bow down to me!" (See Genesis 37:5-11.) That wasn't very smart!

His brothers said, "Forget it! We're not bowing down to you! We hate you!"

(That's the way brothers sometimes talk to each other.) Then Joseph was stupid enough to do it again! He had another dream and did the same thing. Some of his *left* was self-inflicted.

But his dad didn't help matters at all, because he was partially responsible for Joseph going *left*. Jacob's favoritism for Joseph really built up a lot of resentment with his brothers. I would say his *left* was caused both by himself and by his dad's imbalanced relationship with his sons. So Joseph got shoved *left*.

Picture this: here was Joseph walking along, everything was fine, he was wearing his multi-colored coat, and he was singing, "Oh, what a beautiful morning! Oh, what a beautiful day. I've got a beautiful feeling, everything's going my way!" Suddenly, out of the blue, he finds himself chained in a slave convoy on his way to Egypt. It was a rude awakening. He was thinking, "What happened?"

Everything was going fine...and then suddenly, he got shoved *left*. And we're not talking a little bit *left*—he was shoved way *left*! He was totally removed from his family. We can't compare some of our *lefts* to Joseph's *left*. I'm grateful for the *lefts* I've had—but don't give me the "Joseph *left*"! His *left* was totally abysmal.

Joseph Goes *Left* to Egypt

There he was trekking into Egypt in a slave convoy, with chains on his arms, chains on his feet...and he woke up and said, "Hey, I got *left*! What's going on here?"

Sometimes on the *left*, we tend to get in a "pity party." (How would I know that?) Sometimes on the *left*, we tend to vegetate: "It's not going *right* so I'll just park in front of this television...." If it's not going the way we want it to, we retreat. We can't afford to retreat when we are on the *left*.

Joseph went to the *left*, and he ended up in Potiphar's house. What was his behavior like on the *left*, and what did he do that brought him back to the *right*?

> *Now Joseph had been taken down to Egypt. And Potiphar, an officer of Pharaoh,...bought him from the Ishmaelites....The Lord was with Joseph, and he was a successful man;....And his master saw that the Lord was with him and that the Lord made all he did to prosper in his hand....Then he made him overseer of his house, and all that he had he put under his authority. ...the Lord blessed the Egyptian's house for Joseph's sake; and the blessing of the Lord was on all that he had in the house and in the field* (Genesis 39:1-5).

Joseph was *right* with his father in Canaan, then he went *left* with his brothers, and ended up a slave in Egypt. But when he was on the *left*, he was pushed *right* again. In Potiphar's house, he was elevated to a very high position.

Potiphar wasn't some average official. He was very high up in government, very close to Pharaoh, in a very prestigious position. Joseph, the favored son of an Israelite "prince" (that's basically who Jacob was), was shoved out of the *right* into the *left*...and then he was bought as a slave by a man who was very *right* in his own nation.

Now, because he was in a *left* season, Joseph could have had a major pity party. He could have become depressed. Often when we get depressed, we like to sleep, to be lazy, to kick back—we don't want to do anything. But you don't notice that with Joseph.

Joseph wasn't lazy. He could have said, "Okay, I got a really bum rap from my brothers, they totally ripped me off. And now I got dragged down here in this slave convoy; and if you think I'm going to work for you, you're out of your mind. Drop dead. I don't owe you anything." But that wasn't Joseph's mentality. He worked hard.

If you are in a *left* situation, then I challenge you to strive to be recklessly successful on the *left*. If your situation—your kids, your spouse, your job—isn't working *right*, then do everything you know to do to make yourself successful. Make yourself totally invaluable. Work so well that they can't function without you. Do the things that will make you "recklessly successful."

Shooting on the *Left*

When I was growing up, I learned how to shoot the basketball with my right hand—that's because I'm right-handed. But I found out that I also needed to use my left hand. In sports, the very first time we pick up a ball, we use our "natural" hand, and we do well with it. But when we try to use our other hand, it feels kind of awkward.

I once heard of a right-handed high school basketball star who was well on his way to getting a full-ride scholarship to a university to play basketball. However, just before school ended, he broke his right arm and his arm had to be put in a cast for the summer.

All summer long, this young man continued to play basketball, but he used his left hand. In the previous season, many coaches of opposing teams played him on the right side to force him to go *left*, to reduce his effectiveness. During the summer, he only used his left hand. Consequently, when they took the cast off his right arm, the young man had become as skilled with his left hand as he was with his right. When the basketball season started, opposing coaches tried to play the same defense against him, but they were no longer successful, because this young man was equally strong with his left hand as with his right hand. He was virtually indefensible.

How about when we play soccer? If our dominant foot is our right foot, and we try to kick with our left foot, we usually miss the ball and fall down.

Say: "I'm going to be recklessly successful, no matter what!"

Everybody likes to practice on the *right*—we look good, we can shoot, we can dribble, everything's fine—but when we come to the *left*, nobody wants to even try that! Joseph said, "On my *left*, I'm going to do whatever it takes to be recklessly successful"...and God gave him success.

When your life is on the *left*, can you say, "I'm going to work anyway. Okay, so I'm not comfortable, so I'm kind of awkward. So I can't really dribble the ball and I have to watch it all the time. But I'm going to practice, practice, practice! I'm going to be recklessly successful, no matter what. And I'm not going down on the *left*. The *left* isn't going to crush me. I'm going to be successful. Soon I'll be able to shoot with my left hand too, and I'll be awesome at it! I'll be just as good with my *left* as I am with my *right*!"

How about your *left* and your *right*? What is your determination when you're on the *left*? Do you say, "I hate this! This is so bad!"? Come on! I challenge you to be recklessly successful on your *left*.

More of My *Left*

One of the first times I ministered in England, we went to a place that was very, very small. When I was flying over there, I remember thinking, "I've got some good things to share. This is going to be great!" Then I walked in...and there were ten people!

I had a choice. I could just blow that off and say, "Ten people? Forget it! I've preached to crowds of thousands. So I'm going to forget it. I'm not going to bother doing a very good job here." Or—I had a choice to be recklessly successful on the *left*.

How about you? The *left* comes

along...and we back off because we're not comfortable; it's awkward—we don't like it. And then we have the same *left* again and again. But if we practice to be recklessly successful, if we have the determination to be as successful on our *left* as we are on our *right*...then no matter what our *left* is, we will be successful.

Joseph Is *Right* in Egypt

When Joseph went into Potiphar's house he did not have a lot of experience running a household. But he chose to work and do a good job. And look what God did: God blessed him:

> *The Lord was with Joseph, and he was a successful man...and his master saw that the Lord was with him and that the Lord made all he did to prosper in his hand* (Genesis 39:2,3).

God touched him. God prospered him in everything he did.

Two Temptations To Avoid

When we're on the *left*, there are some important things we need to be aware of. On our *left*, it is important to avoid the temptation to blame God. "God, this is Your fault I'm over here speaking to these ten people. I should've just stayed home!" or, "God, this is Your fault that so-and-so died," or "I should have landed that job. God, this is Your fault!" If we blame God, we'll never get to the level of success in our *left* that we desperately need.

Another temptation to avoid, on our *left*, is pushing God away. Often, when we're in challenging times, we just think, "Forget You, God! I'm out of here! I'm pushing You away!" We can't afford to do that. We need Him too much on our *left* to push Him away.

Dad's Little Sister

My father has often told a story that grabs my heart every single time I hear it. When dad was seven he had a little sister who was four years old. She had on this cute little dress...and she was playing with matches. She caught her dress on fire. Dad burned his hands trying to put the fire out. His sister was brutally burned all over her body and eventually she died. It was tragic. We think, "Of all people! An innocent little girl. God, You let people like Hitler live...but she died so young. That's not fair. It's not supposed to be that way."

My grandfather was very upset by his daughter's death. He was just demoralized by it. But my grandmother was wise enough to tell him, "Albert, you can't afford to be mad at God at this time. You need Him too much." In our *left*, we may not be comfortable, we may resent it, we may feel awkward...but we need God too much in our *left* to push away from Him or to blame Him. We will never have reckless success if we exclude God from our *left* times.

A Challenge to You

I want to challenge you when you're in your *left*—look for God. "But Sarah, what do you mean? Is God really in my *left*?" Oh yes, more than we realize, God is in our *left*.

When Joseph was a slave in Potiphar's house, was he complaining? "This is a bum rap. I got dragged all the way down here. I hate this! I'm separated from my family! I want my dad! I'd even tolerate my brothers being around at this time!" No! Joseph put his hand to the plow, he worked hard, he determined, "I'm going to be recklessly successful on my *left*!" Look at what God did!

When you're on your *left*, look for God! What is He doing? When I was going through a very *left* year, I looked for God and I was shocked at what I discovered! God was working in my heart, in my life...on the *left*! How about you? Is God working on you, dealing with you? "Okay, I'm on the *left*, but what is God doing? He's bringing me success and prosperity anyway!"

I was on the *left* that time in England...but I preached with all my might to that audience of ten people. I preached a sermon called "Loosing God," and I put my best effort into it. I could have been even more mad at God because somebody came up and said, "Hmm, it wasn't really that good."

But sometime later I had a pastor come up to me and say, "I used your message about 'Loosing God.' It was phenomenal!" I asked, "Where'd you hear me preach that?" He said, "That first time you came to England."

It's easy to allow *left* situations to scare you off. It's almost as easy (and infinitely more satisfying) to look for what God is *doing* in the midst of the challenge. He IS there!

If you feel like you're perched on

"the edge," put "the edge" to work *for* you—encourage yourself in the Lord, get into His Word, ask Him for a specific scripture you can stand on. When you know Who is on the edge with you, you can forge ahead—FEARLESSLY!

Chapter 3
More *Left* and *Right* for Joseph

Joseph was hanging head-first over the edge when his brothers sold him to be a slave in Egypt, but when he landed in Potiphar's house Joseph started to prosper. God elevated him, basically giving him total control of Potiphar's house. He was doing great. Oh, life was good. He started to sing again, "Oh, what a beautiful morning! Oh, what a beautiful day...."

Suddenly, Potiphar's wife showed up. Out of the blue, he found himself in prison:

> *And it came to pass after these things that his master's wife cast longing eyes on Joseph, and she said, "Lie with me."*

But he refused...as she spoke to Joseph day by day, that he did not heed her, to lie with her or to be with her. ...About this time, when Joseph went into the house to do his work, and none of the men of the house was inside, that she caught him by his garment, saying, "Lie with me."

But he left his garment in her hand, and fled and ran outside....She called to the men of her house and spoke to them, saying, "See, he has brought in to us a Hebrew to mock us. He came in to me to lie with me, and I cried out with a loud voice. And it happened, when he heard that I lifted my voice and cried out, that he left his garment with me, and fled and went outside"....

So it was, when his master heard the words which his wife spoke to him, saying, "Your servant did this to me after this manner," that his anger was aroused. Then Joseph's master took him and put him into the prison,... (Genesis 39:7,10-13,19,20).

Joseph asked, "How'd I get here?" Just because we do the right thing doesn't guarantee that we're going to stay in the *right* place.

Joseph did the right thing. When Potiphar's wife propositioned him to sleep with her, he answered, "I can't do that! I would dishonor my master. I would sin against God. I am not doing that!" He did the right thing. He maintained his integrity. But although he did the right thing, he still got pushed *left*.

Just because we do the right thing doesn't always guarantee we're going to stay in the *right* place. Sometimes we think, "God, I did all of this right—so how come? It's not supposed to be this way!"

God answers, "It's not dependent on you. I'm working on you. I'm dealing with you. I'm changing you. I'm growing you up." If we get shoved *left*, what are we going to do? Back off? Blame God? Be indifferent? Act pathetic? We do the *right* thing, and then we wonder, "Why am I on the *left* for this long time?" We all have *lefts* in our lives—but we cannot afford to stay there.

• First Response to *Left*: Integrity

What did Joseph do *right* while he was on this *left*? What did he say to Potiphar's wife? First, he kept his integrity—he didn't sleep with his master's wife. Sometimes on the *left*, we think, "Aw, nobody's watching. I can get away with this." But that wasn't Joseph's response.

In Australia they have these really huge ranches and they often use helicopters to herd sheep and cattle. They can't manage the herds if they only use trucks, motorcycles, or dogs to move them along. So one day they were using a helicopter to herd some cows, and this one cow got so freaked out that it buried its head in a bush. The rest of the cow was sticking out, but its head was in a bush. The cow thought that because it couldn't see the helicopter, then the helicopter couldn't see it!

Sometimes on the *left*, we act that way, "God can't see me, so I'll do whatever I want to do." No, keep your integrity.

• Second Response to *Left*: Know Your Source

What else did Joseph do *right* while he was on his *left*? He knew the source of his favor. He didn't take the credit himself. He didn't say, "It's my own smart brains and my own good hand that brought me this great position with Potiphar." He knew all along it was God. He knew his Source.

When we're on the *right*, it's a real temptation to think that we're self-made...but when we get on the *left*, we run and say, "God, help me!" On the *right*, we must know Who our Source is...and on the *left,* we must still know Who our Source is. If we don't have that settled and established, we're going to have problems no matter what side we're on, *left* or *right.*

• Third Response to *Left*: Don't Get Bitter

The third thing Joseph did *right* on his *left* was that he didn't get bitter and blame God. He didn't say, "This is Your fault! I'm out of here! You can forget this! Don't even think about using me, God! Forget my integrity, I'm just going to blow this all off! Who cares! This is uncomfortable! I hate this place anyway!" We can't afford to do that.

Joseph's *Left* Was for Others' *Right*

> *But the Lord was with Joseph and showed him mercy, and He gave him favor in the sight of the keeper of*

> *the prison. And the keeper of the prison committed to Joseph's hand all the prisoners who were in the prison;...whatever he did, the Lord made it prosper* (Genesis 39:21-23).

We must realize with Joseph that his *left* was a time of making conditions *right* for other people.

> *And it came to pass after these things that the butler and the baker of the king of Egypt offended their lord, the king of Egypt....He put them in custody in the house of the captain of the guard, in the prison, the place where Joseph was confined.*

> *And the captain of the guard charged Joseph with them,....Then the butler and the baker of the king of Egypt,...had a dream, both of them, each man's dream in one night and each man's dream with*

> *its own interpretation. And Joseph came into them in the morning and looked at them, and saw that they were sad. So he asked... "Why do you look so sad today?"*
>
> *And they said to him, "We each have had a dream, and there is no interpreter of it."...And Joseph said to them, "Do not interpretations belong to God? Tell them to me, please..."*(Genesis 40:1-8).

Joseph talked to the baker and the cupbearer (butler). These two guys were kicked out of Pharaoh's house and sent to prison, and there they had these dreams. Remember: Joseph interpreted dreams. He interpreted for the cupbearer, saying, "You're going to live"—good news! Then he said to the baker, "You're going to die"—bad news.

> *But remember me when it is well with you, and please show kindness*

to me; make mention of me to Pharaoh, and get me out of this house (Genesis 40:14).

So, the cupbearer lived, and Joseph said to him, "Remember me." Where was Joseph when he was asking the cupbearer to remember him? He was on the *left*. It was during Joseph's time on the *left* that he made the provision for the cupbearer's *right*.

It was Joseph's time in Egypt on the *left* that made the provision for his brothers and his family. Don't just think, "I'm on this *left* thing; it's just a character-shaping time for me." Our *left* also makes provision for other people to come on the *right*. It was Joseph on the *left*—learning how to be a good administrator, keeping his integrity, knowing his Source, walking with God, doing the *right* things, being recklessly determined—it was at that time that God was making provision for his family to be on the *right*.

Our *left* is not just for our own

improvement—it is also to make a provision for other people to be on the *right*. When his brothers came to Egypt, was provision made for them? Yes, because Joseph did the things on the *left* that were necessary to have provision on the *right*.

Strong on the *Left* and Strong on the *Right*

> *...I have done nothing here that they should put me into the dungeon"...The chief butler did not remember Joseph...At the end of two full years, Pharaoh had a dream...* (Genesis 40:15, 23; 41:1).

Joseph was in prison, and things were not going well. Did the cupbearer (butler) remember him? No. Two years passed—nothing, no word. There he was, doing the prison administration thing.

Suddenly, he got this call and he went totally from the prison—the gutter, the bottom of the barrel—up to the Pharaoh's house—the "White House," the penthouse, the ultimate of ultimates and once again, Joseph was living on the *right*. Suddenly, it was a massive change.

What enabled him to come strongly to the *right*? It was because he was strong when he was on the *left*.

When we're on our *left*, what are we going to do? Are we going to be recklessly successful, determined? "I don't care what it takes—I'm going to be successful. I'm going to do the best I can on this *left* side." Or are we just going to kick back and quit? It's a choice.

Joseph's *left* was the time of making the provision for other people's *right*.

Our *left* is meant to refine us and improve us, so when we come to the *right*, we've got the guts to stay *right* or to go *left*, and it doesn't crush us on either side.

Chapter 4
Fearless in Pharaoh's House

Before we look at Joseph in Pharaoh's house, let's review his *rights* and his *lefts*. There are some interesting similarities and "coincidences."

What caused Joseph's brothers to envy him? Why did his brothers say, "You're crazy, we'll never serve you!"? How did he get sold into slavery? Joseph told them about his dreams, which sparked hatred in his brothers. Then he was thrown into a pit and sold into slavery. He interpreted dreams for the baker and the cupbearer...but it didn't seem to help his *left* situation.

His integrity also caused him problems. With Potiphar's wife, he kept his integrity, but it still landed him in prison. Joseph must have thought, "If I just would've slept with that lady, I wouldn't be in prison today. If I wouldn't have said anything about those dreams, I might not be here in slavery." But it was his very integrity that caused him to go *left*.

When he was called before Pharaoh, what was he supposed to do? Interpret a dream. Sometimes we think, "I'm not doing this again! I did the *right* thing. I was a person of integrity. I stepped out, used God's giftings and I got crushed because of it. I'm not doing it again."

What would have happened if Joseph had come before Pharaoh and said, "I'm not doing this again. I did the dream thing with my brothers—I got in trouble. I kept my integrity, worked hard, and look at where it got me with Potiphar—in prison. I interpreted the dream for the cupbearer and nothing happened for years! If you think I'm going to interpret your dreams, you're out of your royal mind!"

Sometimes we blame the very gifts that God has given us when we are on the *left*—but those are the keys that will bring us out of the *left* and into the *right*. We can't afford to blame them and Joseph didn't blame them. He wasn't bitter in his heart. We don't read anything in this whole account where he was at all bitter, blaming others, or having a chip on his shoulder. We don't read anything like that.

Payback Time!

> *Then Joseph said to Pharaoh, "The dreams of Pharaoh are one; God has shown Pharaoh what He is about to do....Indeed seven years of great plenty will come throughout all the land of Egypt; but after them seven years of famine will arise, and all the plenty will be forgotten in the land of Egypt; and famine will deplete the land....Now therefore, let Pharaoh select a discerning and wise man, and set him over the land of*

> *Egypt* (Genesis 41:25,28-30,33).
>
> *Then Pharaoh said to Joseph, "Inasmuch as God has shown you all this, there is no one as discerning and wise as you. You shall be over my house, and all my people shall be ruled according to your word; only in regard to the throne will I be greater than you." ...So he set him over all the land of Egypt* (Genesis 41:41,43).

Joseph was an opportunist! He said, "This is a great dream! Pharaoh, you're going to have seven years of plenty, seven years of famine. And I just had this great idea, Pharaoh: you should find some guy who could administrate with integrity, has vision and foresight, who could handle all of the abundance during the years of plenty and famine." Hmm, who could that be? Joseph? What a shock! Those were the very skills God had developed in him while on his *left*.

Six Keys To Surviving the *Left*

Joseph maintained his integrity and still interpreted dreams, even when it seemed like these were the very things that got him into the trouble. Let's see the keys to getting the most out of our *left*.

• First Key: Be Honest With Yourself and Others

God designed us to be people of integrity with Himself, with ourselves, and with other people. We need to maintain our integrity, even on the *left*. We can't bury our heads in the bush and think that God is not watching. God knows what's going on. We need to be people of integrity not only with God, but also with ourselves, being honest and true with ourselves, and true with other people. We must be real persons of integrity.

• Second Key: Don't Neglect God's Orchestrated Gifts

God gave Joseph the gift to interpret dreams. Joseph could have said, "Forget it! It's gotten me nothing but trouble this whole time. Pharaoh, good luck, I wish you well. Live long and prosper. I'm outta here. I'm not doing this!" But he didn't do it. He didn't neglect the gifts that God had given to him.

I know God has given me the gift to teach. But there are times when I honestly think, "God, I don't want to teach! I want to be used in signs and wonders, in healing miracles! Come on, God!"

God says to me again and again, "Sarah, I've given you this gift; don't neglect it. Don't demean it. Don't make it smaller. It's very important. Don't neglect and minimize what I gave you. What I gave you is very important to you."

What are your talents; what are your gifts? Don't just think, "Oh, they're no big deal. They're not important." If God gives them to you, they're extremely important. Don't neglect those things.

• Third Key: Persevere...Press On

It's tempting to think, "Well, I've had a little success on the *left* and that's good enough." Determine in your heart that you're going to be recklessly successful on your *left*. Have dogged determination. When a bulldog bites down on something, its jaws lock, and nothing can pry them open. I challenge you: when you're on the *left*, lock your jaws onto reckless success, and don't give up until you've got it. Have grit and determination. Say, "I'm going to be successful! I don't care if it feels awkward. I'm going to learn how to handle my *left*, so I'll be just as efficient in my *left* as I am with my *right*. I won't be crushed by it. I won't give in to it."

• Fourth Key: Practice Forgiveness

Forgiveness is a key thing for success on our *left*. Look at what happened with the cupbearer. Joseph could have said, "That cupbearer had his dream interpreted two years ago. He didn't say anything to Pharaoh for two years...and I'm just now getting dragged up here? Forget it! He's a loser, you can never trust him. If you think I'm going to interpret Pharaoh's dreams, forget it! This guy is the problem! Just cut his head off." Joseph could have wallowed in unforgiveness and refused to interpret the dreams.

Joseph also had a choice to walk in unforgiveness or forgiveness with his brothers. Personally, there are times when certain people have been directly responsible for my *left*. "It's their fault that I am on the *left*! Those people make me mad!" But I have a choice whether or not I'm going to walk in forgiveness.

There are some ministry situations overseas where I've been shoved *left* and I didn't appreciate that kind of treatment. That is not normal behavior, especially coming from Christians. But we all have a choice when we are on our *left*—to forgive or not. If we don't forgive, we're going to stay on the *left*; in fact, we will get further and more deeply entrenched on the *left*. Our success will get further and further away from us. We cannot afford *not* to forgive on our *left*.

• Fifth Key: Trust God

On the *left*, sometimes we think, "Where did God go?" Sometimes in your prayer time, do you feel like you cry, "God!" and you hear:"GOD!...GOD!...GOD!... GOD..."—kind of an empty echo, and you wonder where He went? Sometimes on the *left*, He seems so far away. But I want to challenge you: step out and trust Him. Walk on the water, trust Him on your *left*! He knows the very hairs on your head. There are times when God seems quiet—yet He's still there.

In the classic "Footprints" poem, the writer reflects on her life—and in the hard times, there is only one set of footprints, so she's mad at God. "Where were You? You are the absent God! ”

God answered, “There’s only the one set of footprints because I was carrying you at those times.” Sometimes when God is quiet, we think He has abandoned us. But remember to look for Him, and trust that He is working in your life.

• Sixth Key: Develop Skills

There are skills we develop in our *left* times which we never even imagined that we needed, could develop, or that even existed. God helps us on our *left*. We learn new things; we see new things. Our *left* times can be very revealing times for us if we will work on developing our skills.

If your spouse is complaining and you’re having a *left* time with your mate, then do the things they’d like for you to do. If you don’t know how to cook, learn how to cook. Develop the skills necessary to improve, so your *left* will be just as strong as your *right*.

Divine Destiny for Living Fearlessly on the Edge

All these keys were necessary for Joseph to fulfill his divine destiny. Joseph needed all of these things—yet all of them were developed on the *left*. How did Joseph get to be overseer in Pharaoh's house? He was determined to be recklessly successful on his *left*. Those skills he developed on his *left* made him so successful on the *right*. It's critical to have them.

Don't be waylaid from your divine destiny.

People are often waylaid from their divine destinies because they don't develop through the *left* times in their lives. It was Joseph's divine destiny to make provision for his brothers and his family. But first it was necessary for him to go through the *left*.

Now here's my challenge to you today: never stand still. If you're in the *left*, declare that, "I'm not stopping in the *left*. I am not ever standing still, I'm always moving. That means I'm going to get so good on my *left* that I can't help but go *right*." We are a moving, growing, increasing people.

> *Blessed is the man whose strength is in You, whose heart is set on pilgrimage* (Psalms 84:5).

We may be on our *left*, but we are going through it. We are not stopping here. If we are in a *left* situation, we must do everything we can do and use all our integrity, so that we take the *right* steps that will take us out of our *left*. Psalm 84:5 means, "I'm not stopped, I'm not staying on the *left*.

What are you going to do with your *left*? What are you going to do when your kids come home and say, "I'm not a Christian. I don't believe in Jesus

Christ." I did that once with my Mom! Talk about *left*! What did Mom do with her *left*? Throw it in? Fight with me? Weep and cry? No!

She held on to God with reckless abandon and tenacity. My mother said, "Okay, that's what you think now. But you're on a pilgrimage, honey, and you're going to come back to Christ." And I did.

What are you going to do with your *left*? If you succumb, if you back off and get wimpy, apathetic, indifferent, or complacent; your *left* will control you, and you will always be a small person.

We determine with reckless abandon to be just as successful on our *left* as we are on our *right*. It doesn't matter which side we're on, we are going to succeed! What are you going to do with your *left*—succeed or fail?

PART TWO
Monuments or Tombstones?

Chapter 5
Road Signs for Edge Travelers

Next we're going to study about how we live according to various signs in our lives. Basically, our lives are governed either by monuments or by tombstones.

For instance, when I'm driving and there's a stop sign, that stop sign tells me to come to a complete stop—not a rolling stop, not a partial stop, not even just an afterthought stop, but a complete stop. That's a sign in my life. We all have signs by which we live our lives. Obeying the law of the land and stopping at stop signs—that's a monument. But oftentimes we live our lives on the edge—by tombstones.

Setting Up Tombstones

We all have issues in our lives; we all have past failures. When I was a child in elementary school, we had Field Day every year. I hated Field Day. I was the slowest person, never jumped the farthest, always was the lowest. In all the competitions, I was the worst. Field Day would come up again every year and would just be terrible. I hated it. That was a tombstone in my life!

Maybe you can identify some things in your life which you've stayed away from. Maybe you were poor in athletics, or had a lack of coordination while growing up. I had a friend who wasn't very good at cooking. When she had the opportunity to serve her in-laws Christmas dinner, she went to a lot of effort to make it...but it was a total failure. It was so bad that when they went to put the spoon into the dressing, they lifted out a Brillo pad! As a result, my friend has not cooked very often from that time. That's a sign in her life—she set up a tombstone.

We all have experiences in our lives that shape us. How often have you said, "I'm never going to do that again"? That's a tombstone. It's a graveyard, a death. "That was a bad thing that happened to me, so I'm never going to do that again."

Oftentimes we don't even realize when we make tombstones. When I was ministering in Norway, a friend of mine was helping translate for me. Privately, she told me, "When I was growing up, I had a friend who never could communicate well with me. It was a struggle for her. She couldn't express herself well. As a result, I was very hurt in that relationship.

"Finally the relationship fizzled out, and I never realized until recently that because that friend hurt me from her poor communication, I had made a silent vow in my heart that I would never be friends with anyone who could not communicate."

That's a death issue, a tombstone. Then she added, "God has revealed to me that I don't have that luxury. I cannot be selective with God's love."

Big and Little Tombstones

We all have past failures. Maybe we made some poor financial decisions, and we say, "I'll never do that again!" Sometimes it's good to learn from failures, but if we live our lives by tombstones, we'll be restricted on how successful and victorious we really are.

When I was trying to learn how to do cartwheels as a child, I just couldn't do them. I wasn't coordinated. Finally I just said, "I will never do another cartwheel ever again." And so I made a silent vow...and that became a little tombstone in my life.

Sometimes we put up tombstones in bigger issues: relationships, financial decisions, our outlook on life, even our Christian witness. Maybe we witnessed to someone but they were rude, so we say, "I'm never going to witness again."

Whether or not we realize it, we set them up and live our lives according to these tombstones. But we don't have to live by tombstones—we can live our lives according to monuments.

Significant Monuments

Monuments are the good things God has done in your life. Monuments are the significant markers in our lives when we absolutely know that God was there, He was making the difference, and we are grateful to Him for that. Sometimes they mark a difficult trial of faith that we endured. They don't always signify "happy" times—sometimes they indicate painful survival. But when God is involved, it is always worth rejoicing... and setting up a monument with thanksgiving.

God wants to help us get resurrection from the tombstones in our graveyards. He wants us to live our lives according to monuments, not by tombstones.

Graveyard Behavior

Most of us don't intentionally set up tombstones. We don't say, "I'm going to be a failure here, so let's set up that tombstone." We never set out to live our lives according to tombstones.

One of the most obvious examples of "graveyard behavior" is shown when the Israelites were wandering in the desert. They wandered in the desert for forty years. Their downfall point came in Numbers chapter 14:

> *So all the congregation lifted up their voices and cried, and the people wept that night. And all the children of Israel complained against Moses and Aaron, and the whole congregation said to them, "If only we had died in the land of Egypt! Or if only we had died*

in this wilderness! Why has the Lord brought us to this land to fall by the sword, that our wives and children should become victims? Would it not be better for us to return to Egypt?" (Numbers 14:1-3).

They complained to God, "We're going to die in the desert!" That was their turning point. They saw nothing but death. They set up tombstones.

Then the Lord said to Moses, "How long will these people reject Me? And how long will they not believe Me, with all the signs which I have performed among them? I will strike them with the pestilence and disinherit them, and I will make of you a nation greater and mightier than they....they certainly shall not see the land of which I swore to their fathers, nor shall any of those who rejected Me see it" (Numbers 14:11,12,23).

God answered, "That's right, you will die." For the next forty years, they wandered in the desert. God said to them, "Not one person of this generation will enter the Promised Land."

For the next forty years, for every person who died, they set up a tombstone. Each time someone died, they'd set up another one, and another one, and another one.

For forty years, they wandered around the desert...and they'd come upon these tombstones and say, "Oh, that's where Aunt Martha died last year." Then they'd come to another tombstone, "Oh, that's where Cousin Reuben died three years ago. Oh, Marian died here, and Eleazar died there"...and soon, the desert became filled with tombstones. They lived their lives within the graveyard.

The exodus from Egypt didn't begin with tombstones, it began with a monument—the Passover. Gradually, however, wrong attitudes produced words of complaint, discouragement, and strife.

If we'll stay focused on the monuments in our lives, we'll guard our hearts with gratitude.

Although they were free from Egypt's grasp, the Israelites were in a self-imposed prison to their own negativity.

We can learn from the Israelites' mistakes. If we'll stay focused on the monuments in our lives, we'll guard our hearts with gratitude. Our words will be gracious and the fruit of our lips, our harvest, will be sweet. Unlike the generation that left Egypt, we *will enter* the Promised Land.

Remember, monuments are reminders of the good things God has done in your life. They serve as springboards to a higher level of success in God!

Chapter 6
Talking Your Way Off the Edge

In Numbers chapter 11, the Israelites started off with "graveyard speech." The way we talk will determine our lifestyle! Whether it's a tombstone lifestyle, or a monument lifestyle—the way we talk determines our outcome.

> *Now the mixed multitude who were among them yielded to intense craving; so the children of Israel also wept again and said, "Who will give us meat to eat? We remember the fish which we ate freely in Egypt, the cucumbers, the melons, the leeks, the onions, and the garlic; but now our whole being is dried up; there is nothing at all except this manna before our eyes!"* (Numbers 11:4-6).

The Israelites came to Moses and complained about the provision God gave them—they were tired of the manna. For goodness' sake, it was heavenly food! They complained and complained...and their words began to create the future. What we say has an effect on where we're going.

The tragic thing is that the Israelites complained to Moses, "We should go back to Egypt. In Egypt, it was so good! We had cucumbers, we had leeks, we had garlic. If only we could go back to Egypt!" Did they really mean that? Didn't they remember that in Egypt they were being beaten and slaughtered? The Egyptians were killing their first-born children! But they complained, "Let us go back to that graveyard of Egypt!" That's exactly what they were saying. They were prophesying their future in a graveyard.

Oftentimes we look at the past, and we think the past is better than the present. "Oh, those were the good old days when...." But if our assessment is that the past was

We look at the past, and we think the past is better than the present.

better than our present, what does that say about our progress?

Our own lives should always be improving, moving, going higher, and getting better. But if we are focused on our tombstones, then the past will always be better than the present. We need to watch carefully what we say. What we say determines our future.

Too Many Complaints

The Israelites were chronic complainers, and so, finally, at the turning point in Numbers chapter 14, God says, "You want to die in the desert, fine! If you want to die, go ahead and speak it into existence."

God was so lenient with them! They complained about the provision for the manna, so God sent them meat. (See Numbers 11:18-20.) They complained about the water, and God said, "Let Moses speak to the rock." (See Numbers 20:8-12.) They complained about their leaders, "Oh, these leaders are so bad!" In Numbers chapter 16, Korah led a revolt against Moses:

> *Now Korah the son of Izhar...with Dathan and Abiram and On...gathered together against Moses and Aaron, and said to them, "You take too much upon yourselves, for all the congregation is holy, every one of them, and the Lord is among them. Why then do you exalt yourselves above the congregation of the Lord?"* (Numbers 16:1-3).

> *When Moses heard it, he fell on his face; and he spoke to Korah and all his company, saying, "...Tomorrow morning the Lord will show who is His and who is holy, and will cause him to come near to Him..."* (Numbers 16:5).

> *Now it came to pass, as he finished speaking all these words, that the ground split apart under them, and the earth opened its mouth and swallowed them up, with their households and all the men with Korah, with all their goods. So they and all those with them went down alive into the pit; the earth closed over them, and they perished from among the congregation* (Numbers 16:31-33).

As a result of Korah's insurrection, hundreds of people died in one day. Picture that graveyard! Imagine the tombstones for all those dead people! They prophesied it with their mouths ahead of time. They spoke death, and so then they lived in death. Even after the Korah incident, the Israelites still lived their lives by the signs of the tombstones, and they kept complaining. Later we read that a plague killed another 14,700 people. (See Numbers 16:41-50.)

They complained about their future—and so they compromised their future. Later, they compromised by intermarrying with the Midianites. God never intended for them to intermarry—He intended for them to be their own nation. By intermarrying, they compromised their future. The result of this intermarrying was the death of 24,000 people in one day. (See Numbers 25.) Talk about a big graveyard: 24,000 people—24,000 tombstones!

Although they were the children of God's promise, the Israelites lived their lives according to tombstones. They prophesied death into their future.

Tombstone Reflections

Do our words reflect a "tombstone" or "monument" lifestyle? Are we fearless on the edge or living in a graveyard? We don't want to miss God's purpose, His intention, for our lives. God never meant for us to be walking cadavers. He breathed into us to give us life—resurrection life, life abundantly:

> *...I have come that they may have life, and that they may have it more abundantly* (John 10:10).

> *Jesus said to her, "I am the resurrection and the life. He who believes in Me, though he may die, he shall live"* (John 11:25).

God has not called us to live a tombstone lifestyle.

Chapter 7
Power Symbols for the Fearless

Now let's look at a special individual in the Bible who set up monuments to the good things God did in his life. Monuments are power symbols for the fearless and exhibit the benefits of living life in a godly manner.

Lions and Bears...and Giants!

David was constantly setting up monuments, and pointing them out to people:

> *Then David said to Saul, "Let no man's heart fail because of him*

> [Goliath]*; your servant will go and fight with this Philistine." And Saul said to David, "You are not able to go against this Philistine to fight with him; for you are a youth, and he a man of war from his youth."*
>
> *Your servant has killed both lion and bear; and this uncircumcised Philistine will be like one of them, seeing he has defied the armies of the living God." Moreover David said, "The Lord, Who delivered me from the paw of the lion and from the paw of the bear, He will deliver me from the hand of this Philistine." And Saul said to David, "Go, and the Lord be with you!"* (I Samuel 17:32,33,36,37).

When David first heard the challenge to go up against Goliath, everyone else around him was freaked out, "Oh no, the guy's going to kill us! We can't do this!"

But what did David say? "Hey, no

problem! I killed a lion, I killed a bear, and this guy's not going to be a problem for me either." He had a mental monument, a picture in his mind of what God had done for him. And he pointed it out to Saul. We need to reflect on the monuments which God has given us to live our lives fearlessly.

Find a Mental Monument

I remember when I first started preaching overseas. Mom gave me the privilege of sharing for a whole evening in Bulgaria, and I loved it. Before the service, the translator and I were discussing the message, and he said, "Okay, we're going to do well, we're going to be fine." Then he asked me, "Oh, by the way, how many times have you ministered overseas and used a translator?"

I answered, "None."

He sort of chuckled, then said, "No, really, how many times have you done this?"

I looked at him and said, "None. Zero."

He seemed really uptight, but said: "Oh well, we'll be fine, don't you worry about it." *He* was nervous...but *I* wasn't apprehensive at all. When I got up to speak, I honestly felt like I was born to do that. I felt like a fish in water! It was as if I had been doing it my entire life. At that point, I established a mental monument to God's gift to me.

I was having a good time, thinking, "Wow, God is doing great things!" But when we called for testimonies about the miracles, it was a total dead end. Nobody came forward with any testimonies! I was really out on a limb! I had prayed for different healings—injured backs, other illnesses—but no one came forward with testimonies.

I prayed, "God, confirm Your Word!" I kept returning to my mental monument of God's goodness. I kept persevering. I looked at my translator, "Anything else we should pray about?

Any other sicknesses that are common here?"

He mumbled, "I don't know what to do."

So I said, "Well, let's keep on praying." So we did...and eventually it broke, and we had some of the best testimonies! There was a lady who hadn't been able to bend over for twenty years, who had undergone multiple surgeries. She came forward and, for the first time in twenty years, she could bend over without pain. This was my first time to do this! For me, that was a mental monument.

What has God done for you? "Well, He hasn't done anything...." Of course He has! It's His goodness that draws us, sustains us, motivates us! We all need to reflect on some of the mental monuments, the good things God has given us in our lives that reflect His goodness to us. These are the signs in our lives—not a stop sign, not a yield sign, not a speed limit—but mental monuments by which we can keep moving, going, progressing, so our past doesn't defeat us.

Carry It With You

Let's consider another monument David found, a mobile monument.

> *Now David came to Nob, to Ahimelech the priest. And Ahimelech was afraid when he met David, and said to him, "Why are you alone, and no one is with you?"* (I Samuel 21:1).

> *And David said to Ahimelech, "Is there not here on hand a spear or a sword? For I have brought neither my sword nor my weapons with me...." So the priest said, "The sword of Goliath the Philistine, whom you killed in the Valley of Elah, there it is, wrapped in a cloth behind the ephod. If you will take that, take it. For there is no other*

except that one here." And David said, "There is none like it; give it to me." (I Samuel 21:8,9).

David went to see the priest Ahimelech, who had kept Goliath's sword in the temple. David said, "Look, I'm on the run. I'm running from Saul, and I need a sword. So do you have a sword here?"

Ahimelech answered, "Well, the only sword I have is Goliath's sword."

David exclaimed, "Whoa! There's no sword like that!" David took that sword (it was now his sword anyway, since he had defeated Goliath), and that sword became a mobile monument. He took it with him.

Carry something with you to reflect God's victory in your life.

Sometimes we need to take something with us to reflect God's victory in our lives. When we come against those difficult situations that want to speak death, defeat, total despair—pull out that mobile monument, and say, "Look at what God did here, here, and here...and what is He going to do now?"

We all carry things with us all the time. Men carry wallets; women carry purses; some of us carry briefcases. What mobile monuments can we carry with us all the time? We need to carry constant encouragements to live in life.

I know of a woman who always carries a very dog-eared photograph of herself in the hospital when she was undergoing chemotherapy. Her head was bald, her skin was mottled, her eyes were sunken, there were tubes hooked up to her all over the place. But she was smiling. She looked cheerful. She wasn't afraid. And God healed her completely!

Now all her hair is grown back, she looks radiant and healthy. She has been declared cancer-free for over ten years. She pulls out that photograph and shows it to people, saying, "Look at what God did for me. I was dying of cancer. It was eating me up. Medical science was doing all it could for me, but my Lord Jesus Christ is the One Who made the difference. He healed me when the doctors said they couldn't help me anymore." That photograph is her mobile monument.

Another woman I know had open-heart surgery, which left a big, ugly, puckered scar from her throat to her navel. She would pull down the neck of her blouse a few inches and declare (sometimes to complete strangers), "See this scar? I had open-heart surgery. But Jesus Christ has healed me. I am a walking miracle." She wasn't ashamed. That was her mobile monument.

David's Miracle Monument

The third monument that David set up is in I Samuel chapter 26—it was a miracle monument:

> *So David and Abishai came...by night; and there Saul lay sleeping ...with his spear stuck in the ground by his head. And Abner and the people lay all around him. Then Abishai said to David, "God has delivered your enemy into your hand this day. Now therefore, please, let me strike him at once with the spear, right to the earth; and I will not have to strike him a second time!"*
>
> *And David said to Abishai, "Do not destroy him; for who can stretch out his hand against the Lord's anointed, and be guiltless?...The Lord forbid that I should stretch out my hand against the Lord's anointed. But please, take now the spear and the jug of water that are by his head, and let us go."* (I Samuel 26:7-9,11,12).

This was a miracle monument to God's anointing. David refused to hurt Saul because of the anointing on Saul's life. David knew that God had anointed Saul, and that He had anointed David. The miracle-working power of God had come upon Saul, and was coming on David.

He said, "God anointed Saul, so I'm not going to touch him. I am going to be very careful, considerate, and mindful of this anointing. I am going to protect it because I have the same anointing on my life."

When has God done a miracle for you? I love thinking of the miracles He's done for me. I reflect often on the miracle of life: scientists say that the probability of a sperm and an egg uniting is very, very small. We all are walking miracles. But do we live our lives as monuments or as tombstones?

God meant for us to be miracles, to be monuments, so we need to live accordingly. We very easily identify tombstones in our lives, but I want to tell you: for the tombstones, the graveyards of our lives, God has resurrection!

Chapter 8
Life on the Edge

Let's look at one giant graveyard, and see what God said about it:

The hand of the Lord came upon me and brought me out in the Spirit of the Lord, and set me down in the midst of the valley; and it was full of bones. Then He caused me to pass by them all around, and behold, there were very many in the open valley; and indeed they were very dry. And He said to me, "Son of man, can these bones live?" So I answered, "O Lord God, You know."

Again He said to me, "Prophesy to these bones, and say to them, 'O dry bones, hear the word of the Lord! Thus says the Lord God to these bones: Surely I will cause breath to

> *enter into you, and you shall live. I will put sinews on you and bring flesh upon you, cover you with skin and put breath in you; and you shall live. Then you shall know that I am the Lord.'"*
>
> *So I prophesied as I was commanded; and as I prophesied, there was a noise, and suddenly a rattling; and the bones came together, bone to bone* (Ezekiel 37:1-7).

In Ezekiel chapter 37, God took Ezekiel in a vision to a valley. He said, "Ezekiel, what do you see?" He made Ezekiel walk around, and he saw he was walking in a valley of dry bones.

Sometimes our lives feel like a valley of dry bones. Maybe we're like the Israelites with 40,000 tombstones in one spot. Maybe our lives are full of skeletons. Our lives seem to be a dry, desolate, empty valley—just full of bones.

In the early 1970's, there was a

political group called the Khmer Rouge, who massacred thousands and thousands in Cambodia, in what they called "the killing fields." Proportionately, they killed more innocent people in Cambodia than were killed in the Holocaust during World War II. The killing fields were literally a massively huge field of bones.

For some of us, that's like our lives. We live in such failure, such defeat. Everywhere we step: another bone, another grave, another tombstone. But God wants us to know that He has resurrection for our valleys of dry bones.

Three Important Questions

God asks Ezekiel a few questions—and those questions are our steps to resurrection! First, God asked him, "Look down, what do you see?"

Ezekiel replied, "I see a valley of dry bones."

For us to have resurrection, we must first acknowledge where there's death. Ask yourself, "Where are the tombstones?" Identify the death issues in your life. "What are things that I have lived according to death, sometimes for a long, long time?" These issues keep us back; they impede us. If we don't identify them, how will we ever have resurrection?

Maybe we have past hurts. Perhaps you were betrayed, and you say, "I'll never trust anyone again." That's a tombstone. I understand fully about learning from past mistakes, but there's a difference between learning from them and living by them. So identify the tombstones, identify the dead areas.

The second question that God asked him was, "Can these bones live?" This is the God Who made the entire universe, asking mere man, "Can these bones live?"

When we look at the issues of death, of tombstones in our lives, God asks each of

Life can flow from what was once death.

us, "Can these bones live? Can your tombstones live?"

Ezekiel was pretty convinced about it, "Yes, Lord, I think You can make these bones live." If we want resurrection, then we need to believe in God's life-giving power. If we don't believe that our tombstones can be overturned and life can flow from what once was death, then we're wasting our time. If we don't believe that God has life for us, then we never get resurrection.

The third thing that God asked of Ezekiel was, "Prophesy to the bones." Speak to the dead issues in our lives. Speak life to the bones!

That's exactly what Ezekiel did. He said, "When God told me to speak life, I did. I spoke to the bones, saying, 'Bones, come together! Bones, get a life!'"

We must say to our bones, "Have life!" We must prophesy to the dead areas of our lives, "Have resurrection life!"

Rattling Bones

The moment Ezekiel prophesied, those bones started to rattle. Put yourself in Ezekiel's shoes: he was walking around in this valley with all these dry bones...then he prophesied, "Have life, come together!"...and suddenly these bones started to rattle.

In the original Hebrew, it wasn't just "rattle." Those bones made a monstrous sound. As we speak God's word to the dead areas in our lives, we're going to hear things start to rattle, shake, move, and come together. It will be awesome!

A friend was telling me about one of his kids who was running around, really doing bad things. He said, "I was so discouraged. But then I started to hear what I myself was saying about my son...and instead of complaining and moaning, I started to speak life. I began to say, 'He's not going to behave that way. In fact, he's going to be sick of sin, he's going to become revolted by it. It's going to disgust him...and he's going to have a passion for God.'" What happened? The "bones" started to come together. There's been a change, a turnaround in that kid's life, because his father "spoke life."

Resurrection Life

The Bible says that the bones came together—bone to bone...the sinews came together...and flesh came on the bones—but they still did not have life:

> *So I prophesied as I was commanded; and as I prophesied, there was a noise, and suddenly a rattling; and the bones came together, bone to bone. Indeed, as I looked, the sinews and the flesh came upon them, and the skin covered them over; but there was no breath in them.*

> *Then He said to me, "Prophesy to the breath, prophesy, son of man, and say to the breath, 'Thus says the Lord God: Come from the four winds, O breath, and breathe on these slain, that they may live."*
>
> *So I prophesied as He commanded me, and breath came into them, and they lived, and stood upon their feet, an exceedingly great army* (Ezekiel 37:7-10).

God said again, "Speak life to the bones." We get a little happiness, we get a little bit of success...and we think that's enough. But bones are still cadavers without the life of God in them. We must continue to speak, to prophesy life into the dead areas of our lives. If we don't want to live by tombstones, then we must speak life.

Ezekiel said, "All right, I'll keep doing it." As he prophesied the second time, the wind came, breathed on them, and turned all that valley of dead, dry bones into a live army.

God has a mighty army in our dry bones. God has function, purpose, and intention for us in our valley of dry bones—from those tombstones, and from the death in our lives. God wants to make us a mighty army to advance His kingdom.

God has life for us to speak to our tombstones. Now that we've identified the dead issues in our lives, we have to begin speaking life to those issues. Say, "You're not dead—this issue, this friendship, this hurt, this financial disaster—I speak life to you now."

> *I shall not die, but live, and declare the works of the Lord* (Psalms 118:17).

God never intended for those tombstones to remain tombstones. God has resurrection for us in our tombstones.

The problem with the Israelites is that they prophesied death with their mouths. They complained about provision, complained about their future, and they prophesied their death.

So what are we saying about the future? What are we saying about the past? "They did me wrong!" Maybe they did, but can God bring resurrection out of the wrong? Absolutely! That is God's business—turning the negative into the positive. Isaiah 61:3 reads;

> *...To give them beauty for ashes, the oil of joy for mourning, the garment of praise for the spirit of heaviness; that they may be called trees of righteousness, the planting of the Lord, that He may be glorified.*

That's exactly what God does. He takes your garbage, and gives you His glory. He's in the exchange business. But will we let Him bring resurrection? Will we speak and prophesy to our tombstones? Live, and not die? That's what we have to do.

God's Kind of Monument

When it comes to divine monuments, God gave us a wonderful example:

> *And God said, "This is the sign of the covenant which I make between Me and you, and every living creature that is with you, for perpetual generations: I set My rainbow in the cloud, and it shall be a sign of the covenant between Me and the earth.*
>
> *"It shall be, when I bring a cloud over the earth, that the rainbow shall be seen in the cloud; and I will remember My covenant which is between Me and you and every living creature of all flesh; the waters shall never again become a flood to destroy all flesh. The rainbow shall be in the cloud, and I will look on it*

> *to remember the everlasting covenant between God and every living creature of all flesh that is on the earth." And God said to Noah, "This is the sign of the covenant which I have established between Me and all flesh that is on the earth"* (Genesis 9:12-17).

God believes in establishing monuments, to help us rule our lives His way. His kind of monument is visible, beautiful, and eternal. Monuments to God's ruling in your life will be a sign to others who are on the edge. Let God resurrect your tombstones, your dead bones.

PART THREE

Turning Mud Into Miracles

Chapter 9
The Soil of Deliverance

We all have dirt in our lives. Some people have dirt that revolves around addictions—sex addicts, drug addicts, food addicts, TV addicts, Internet addicts. Some addictions can be so overwhelming that we think there's no hope and we want to give up. Addictions are terrible, binding things that can hurt and destroy lives.

Other people have the dirt of depression, some have paranoia. Some people have dirt in their lives from the hurt from past relationships. Others come out of abusive backgrounds, where they were physically or verbally abused. When there is sexual abuse, people walk around with this dirt in their lives, and they begin to believe that they themselves are dirty. Some people have physical infirmities, and that is dirt in their lives. God has a lot to say about dirt...and He's been known to use mud as a means for bringing miracles into dirty lives.

A Miracle in That Mud!

There are steps that Jesus walks us through to get our miracle. We don't have to live in the dirt, but can be "kissed" by the divine and experience miracles. Let's start with what Jesus did in John chapter 9:

> *Now as Jesus passed by, He saw a man who was blind from birth. When He had said these things, He spat on the ground and made clay with the saliva; and He anointed the eyes of the blind man with the clay. And He said to him, "Go, wash in the pool of Siloam".... So he went and washed, and came back seeing* (John 9:1,6,7).

John chapter 9 told about a gentleman who was in the dirt, who had a physical infirmity—a need in his life. There were steps that Jesus led him through to meet his need, to make and multiply the miracle. Often we have the perspective, "I need the miracle for me"—when in actuality, God needs the miracle for everyone else.

Miracles may be for us, but they are rarely *just* for us—they are often to be multiplied for the masses. When we receive miracles in our lives, we are changed and are to be demonstrable miracles. When people see us after a miracle, they say, "What happened?" We will be walking miracles—demonstrating the turnaround in our lives. There are two important steps to becoming one of God's miracles.

Step One: "What's Under the Dirt?"

The Bible says that Jesus saw a man who was born blind. The first step to turn our mud into a miracle is to identify the core problem—recognize what is wrong. Oftentimes we look at the abuse in our lives and we think that's the problem. We look at the addiction in our lives and we think that's the problem. In actuality, there's something behind those actions, those behaviors that is motivating that dirt. For instance, alcoholism might be a symptom of bitterness and it is the bitterness we need to face.

When Jesus saw the blind man, He didn't just walk up to him and say, "Hey, how's it going? I see that you're blind. Well, I just hope you live long and prosper." No! He was very attentive to what was going on with this man. He didn't just acknowledge the obvious problem—He wanted to know the core causes.

Jesus asked him, "What's wrong?" He wasn't saying, "What are your symptoms?" but He was saying, "What is the core of your problem?" It wasn't just the symptoms—not just alcoholism or addictions—but the source of the illness, of the dirt. Don't treat the symptoms when you can go for the source! That's exactly what Jesus said, "What's wrong? I don't want to know the symptoms, obviously you're blind. But I want to get to the core, to the source."

Jesus asks us, "What's wrong?" Maybe we have abusive behavior, addictions, or physical needs. Maybe it's something passed from generation to generation. Jesus asks us, "What is the source? What is the driving, fundamental basis for your dirty or sick behavior?"

Step Two: "Moving Beyond 'Why'"

The second step for our miracle is to realize "why." Jesus' disciples asked Him, "Hey, why did this happen? What's the reason? Was it because his parents sinned, or was it because he sinned?" Oftentimes as humans, we will identify what's wrong—we'll get to the source—

but then our next question is, "Why did this happen?"

We ask God, "Why am I sick?" "Why, Father, did You not protect me from being abused when I was growing up?" "Why did You stand and watch this?" "Why?" As humans, we often never progress beyond, "Why?" But God can make a miracle out of our mud if we will move past the "Why?"

Knowing "why" doesn't cure you.

The disciples asked this question of Jesus when they said, "Who sinned?" Jesus' answer to their question is the same answer He gives us—knowing "why" doesn't cure you. The cure comes when you accept Jesus' power to bring change, transformation, and the miraculous into your life.

We are to be walking miracles and our miracles are meant to witness to the masses! Our miracles are to be multiplied!

Chapter 10
Spitting Over the Edge

Our first two steps for turning our mud into miracles were to ask ourselves "what is the core of the problem and why does God allow it in our lives?" Jesus told His disciples that the blind man was blind—that's the "what." It was so his healing could reveal God's glory—that's the "why." God's glory can be revealed through our dirt! Isn't that amazing?

"Sam" and the Truck Driver

I know a gentleman—we'll call him "Sam"—who came out of a very abusive background. His father abused him terribly, beating him almost daily. The longer Sam suffered this abuse, the more angry he became.

By the time Sam entered his early teens, he was so angry that he ran away from home and became a violent, destructive, clearly abusive person. The older he got, the worse he became. Because of his own abusive background, he left a path of destruction behind him. He was in trouble with the law. When he got married, he abused his wife. When he had kids, he wanted to abuse them. He was about to repeat a horrible pattern of abuse.

Eventually, Sam contemplated suicide. Then Jesus brought a miracle into his life—made his mud into a miracle. While Sam was walking down a road, thinking about killing himself, a truck driver drove up behind him, stopped, and said, "Look, God put you on my heart to take you to the church at the next exit." The truck driver took Sam to the church (which just happened to be our church, Orchard Road Christian Center), and he walked in, and was dramatically, and radically saved! Do you believe that God has a miracle for you in your mud?

Later, I talked with him, and Sam said, "I would often ask God, 'Why was I abused when I was growing up? Why did You let this happen? Why did You stand there silently, and by Your non-involvement agree to let this happen?'" Sam wrestled with this, and had a hard time with it. He was struggling and looking for answers when God finally spoke to him.

God answered Sam, "I brought you this far—through the abuse, into the victorious life—so that you can be a miracle for others, so that the glory of God can be revealed through you." That was the "why" for Sam. Often we get mired in the mud of "why" and we never get out of it. We never free ourselves. Jesus' answer for us is: "So that God's glory can be revealed through you."

> *He also brought me up out of a horrible pit, out of the miry clay, and set my feet upon a rock, and established my steps* (Psalms 40:2).

Making More Mud

Let's review how Jesus healed the blind man—and also see how He will heal us! Jesus was not into methodology, not into formula, not into "typical" behavior:

> *When He had said these things, He spat on the ground and made clay with the saliva; and He anointed the eyes of the blind man with the clay. And He said to him, "Go, wash in the pool of Siloam".... So he went and washed, and came back seeing* (John 9:6,7).

Jesus spat in the dirt, made mud (or "clay"), and put it on the guy's eyes. "Wait a minute! That's disgusting! That's revolting!" Well, those are our standards—but Jesus wasn't into our standards. He was operating on a supernatural level that was way beyond our "standards."

Nevertheless, the man didn't back off and say, "Don't do that! I'm going to get a disease from Your saliva!" He let Jesus touch him. Jesus took the dirt, spat in it, mixed it with the "divine"...and the man had a miracle.

We get so fixated on "the dirt." "What kind was it? Did Jesus know about some special herbal remedy? Was the dirt actually a very fine sand, and when he put it on the guy's eyes, it scraped away the cataracts or something?" None of these! The dirt was just dirt—ordinary, every day dirt. The healing came from Jesus.

Jesus' Healing Power

We already know about some of the wonderful saving and healing properties of Jesus' body.

> *Whoever eats My flesh and drinks My blood has eternal life, and I will raise him up at the last day* (John 6:54).

> *But He was wounded for our*

> *transgressions, He was bruised for our iniquities; the chastisement for our peace was upon Him, and by His stripes we are healed* (Isaiah 53:5).

> *Who Himself bore our sins in His own body on the tree, that we, having died to sins, might live for righteousness—by whose stripes you were healed* (I Peter 2:24).

John chapter 9 tells us that Jesus had healing power, even when He chose to apply His spit. Jesus wants to come into our dirt, spit in it, mix it with the divine, and give us our miracle. He has a miracle for us in our dirt, in our infirmity, in our sickness, in the abuse, in the stuff that mires us. Are you on the edge of a miracle?

Now it seemed like the man became worse before he became better. He was blind, and now, in addition to being blind, he had mud on his eyes.

Why would we think that just "the mud" would make him suddenly get better? He went from "just plain blind" to "blind with mud"—from bad to worse. Sometimes it seems like we literally get worse before we get better. But God has a miracle for us in the mud.

Created To Work Perfectly

Jesus wanted to take the man's blind eyes and bring them back to their original purpose. Jesus never intended for the man to live in blindness.

Our eyes were meant to see. By design, our ears were made to hear. Our hearts were designed to love. Our minds, our souls were meant to know truth.

When dirt comes in, it distorts and warps. Our eyes become blind from the dirt, our ears become deaf from the dirt, our hearts become numb and hard from the dirt. Our minds become depressed, paranoid and all kinds of bizarre things happen because of the dirt. That's not why we were created. We were created to function in perfection.

> *So God created man in His own image; in the image of God He created him; male and female He created them* (Genesis 1:27).

God made man out of dirt. He got into the dirt, shaped it, molded it. The scripture in Hebrew literally says: "He took the dirt and sculpted it." He shaped and molded and sculpted it to look like a man.

> *And the LORD God formed man of the dust of the ground, and breathed life into his nostrils the breath of life, and man became a living being* (Genesis 2:7).

Nevertheless, without the divine, it's still dirt. So what did He do to the dirt? The Bible says, "He breathed on it and it had life" (Genesis 2:7). It was the divine touch on the dirt that turned it into the perfect man, Adam. God wants to come back into our dirt, take that hardship, touch it with the divine, and make a miracle.

We don't have to live in the dirt. Jesus has a miracle for us in our mud. Not only are our eyes meant to see, our ears meant to hear, our hearts meant to love, and our minds meant to know truth, but Jesus also says, "Look, I want to touch the dirt for you. I want to mix it with the divine and give you a miracle."

Walk It Out

And He said to him, "Go, wash in the pool of Siloam" (which is translated, Sent). So he went and washed, and came back seeing (John 9:7).

In John 9:7, we discover that the man has to connect with the mud. We often want to avoid our dirt. It's too real in our lives. But Jesus says, "If you do what I tell you to do, if you mix the dirt with the divine and combine your faith with it, then you'll have your miracle."

Jesus told the blind man to do two things: "go" and "wash"—keys to his miracle. Faith works; faith takes action. Miracles require that we engage and connect.

Look at Jesus' first command: "Go." What happened with this man when Jesus told him, "Go"? The man was blind! How was he going to go? Was the pool just around the corner? The man was blind, now he had mud on his eyes—how was he supposed to go? He had to walk there, take action.

Let's give the man the benefit of the doubt and say that he knew how to get to the pool of Siloam to wash. Everyone in that city knew him to be a blind beggar. Now they saw him walking...but they didn't just see him walking blind or aimlessly—they saw him walking, doing, going with purpose! They saw him taking action, making the connection, having faith, showing movement. They didn't just see him going—they saw him going with mud on his eyes!

Now put yourself in his shoes: how would you feel? First, you're blind—that's kind of a drawback to start with. Now, you're a spectacle. Everybody sees you and laughs, "Hey, what's with that mud on your eyes?"

Think about how cruel children can be: "Look at that man! What's that crazy man doing?"

You can just hear the women: "Oh, does he have that new herbal remedy I've heard about, that Dead Sea mud ointment? Wow, let's go try that!"

That blind man was a walking testimony of "before-and-after." Everyone saw him—he was standing out, he was blatant. If we went to a shopping mall and saw someone walking by with mud on their eyes, wouldn't we be whispering, "What in the world? He's a walking spectacle!"

Often we want a private miracle.

We want to be in the closet because we don't want our dirt known to everybody. We don't want to be obvious. But we don't have that luxury if we need a miracle.

What happened once the blind man got to the pool? He would need help. He would need someone to come alongside him, someone he could hold on to, someone to lead him into the pool.

Oftentimes we lack our miracles because we won't let people help us. People hurt us, and so we back away, "No, you hurt me! I can do this on my own!" That is blindness. We have mud on our eyes, and we keep running into things because we won't let people help us. Jesus has a miracle for us whether we know how to get it or not. He wants to bring the divine into our dirt and help us to walk it out.

Action Time

In our lives, we must first identify the "whats"—the core issues affecting our lives. Maybe we came out of abusive backgrounds, maybe we're angry. Maybe we're addicted to food because we're depressed. Maybe we're bitter, walking in unforgiveness, and that is causing us to hurt others.

God wants to use us for His glory.

We have already moved beyond the "why" because we know God wants to use us for His glory. Now we're going to let Christ come into our dirt, into the problems of our lives, into our sicknesses, to touch us. Now the question is: "What is God telling us to do?" Whatever He wants us to do, that's what we need to do. If we want to have our miracles, then we have to walk them out.

What if our core issue is anger? Maybe we are angry from failed relationships. Maybe God is telling us to get into a healthy relationship with someone for accountability. We often desire a miracle, but we're not willing to walk it out. God wants us to identify our dirt and walk out a miracle.

What about lack of trust? Maybe we don't trust people—we've been hurt, so we don't trust anyone. Maybe God's direction is to go for counseling. What is God asking us to do? There's no washing, no getting rid of the dirt until we first have action, until we first "Go."

Next, Wash It Off

This blind man went to the pool, and obeyed Jesus. He said, "Okay, no matter what it takes me to get to this pool, even if I have to look like a fool, I'm going." He went and he washed. When he washed, what happened? He washed the mud off, he got rid of the dirt...and he was left with the divine! He could see! That's exactly what God wants us to do—to wash off the dirt and get our miracle!

These are the action steps we must take. There's a step for "go" (that's motion), there's a step to get help, and then there's a step for "wash"—a step to let it go, to leave it in the past. Often we'll go and be involved in doing, but we neglect to wash, to leave it in the past. That's often where we miss our miracle—we hold on, we rehearse, we review the past. We have to get over it.

God says, "You've already put your faith into action. You're moving, that's excellent! Now it's time to wash off the dirt and leave it back there." Sam had been abused. He went, he received help, and he got a miracle in the mud. Then he washed off the dirt. By washing off the dirt, he left it in the past...and now Sam is a functioning minister of God, reaching other individuals who have been abused. But he would never be at that point if he didn't wash it off.

Let it go.

Chapter 11
Multiplied Miracles on the Edge

This blind man in John chapter 9 really is a great example for us. His story shows us how God wants to take our dirt, make divine mud out of it, and give us our miracle. Now, the next thing we're going to see is the *multiplied miracle*. I would say to you—in fact, I would challenge you—if your miracle isn't yet multiplied, it's still mud by comparison to what it could be.

> *...Those who previously had seen that he was blind said, "Is not this he who sat and begged?" Therefore they said to him, "How were your eyes opened?" He answered and*

> *said, "A Man called Jesus made clay and anointed my eyes and said to me, 'Go to the pool of Siloam and wash.' So I went and washed, and I received sight* (John 9:8,10).

This blind man received his healing. He walked away from the Pool of Siloam and he could see. Everyone who saw him before—when he was a spectacle with mud on his eyes—could see that his eyes were totally open. He could see. He was a walking testimony.

A Public Miracle

Those people were shocked! "Hey, aren't you the man who sat and begged?"..."Are you the man who was blind?"..."No, that's not him"..."Yes, it is!" They kept going back and forth.

Finally he said, "Yes, I'm the one." Those people saw the "before." Now they saw him walking and they said, "He's a miracle! What happened?" He was a miracle for his community.

Jesus means for us to be miracles for our communities. He wants us to be the before-and-after testimonies. People around us see our sicknesses. Oftentimes we think that people don't really know how sick we are—they do. We're not deceiving anyone, just ourselves.

They Couldn't See It

Jesus not only means for us to be miracles for our communities, but also for the leaders in our lives. The people of His community took the formerly blind man to the leaders.

> *They brought him who formerly was blind to the Pharisees. Now it was a Sabbath when Jesus made the clay and opened his eyes....Therefore some of the Pharisees said, "This Man is not from God, because He does not keep the Sabbath." Others said, "How can a Man Who is a*

> *sinner do such signs?" ...He answered and said, "Whether He is a sinner or not I do not know. One thing I know: that though I was blind, now I see"* (John 9:13-16,25).

The Pharisees badgered the man because his testimony baffled their religious minds. This Jesus had not only presumed to heal someone, but He chose to do it *on the Sabbath*! The blind man was not interested in finding a rationale for what had happened. As far as he was concerned, healing was an obvious "God thing," regardless of *when* it was done.

The healed man kept telling them, "This is what happened: I was blind, now I see! Who did it, why He did it, how He did it...I don't know. All I know is: I was blind, now I see! Get it?"

Isn't that just the way many people react? If they can't hold it in their hands and dissect it, they refuse to believe it. If they can't duplicate it, they discount it. The Pharisees really gave this ex-blind man a hard time because they couldn't rationalize what had happened.

Finally they said, "Well, tell us once more."

He was so fed up with them, he said, "Look, do you want to believe and become a convert?" Do you catch what's happening here? It's the multiplied miracle. Not just for us—but for our community, for the leaders in our lives.

The Pharisees Were "Blind"

The Pharisees didn't believe him. "You weren't blind from birth."

He retorted, "Yes, I was."

"Prove it!" So the man brought his family. God wants us to be walking miracles for our families too. Here came Mom and Dad. Not only had he become a miracle for the community, not only had he become a miracle for the leadership...now he was a miracle for his family. God wants us to be miracles for our families—and we know that sometimes our closest family members can be the harshest critics.

So the parents reported, "Yes, he was born blind. We don't know how he became healed, but he was born blind." The ex-blind man witnessed to his parents—the multiplied miracle. Again, I would say: if our miracle is not multiplied, by comparison it's still mud. Maybe we had a touch of the divine, but when we multiply it, that's when the miracle becomes explosive, growing, and reproducing. That's exactly what God's kingdom is about: reproducing miracles in others.

Making a Divine Exchange

We've talked about the dirt in our lives. We've discussed moving beyond "why." We've seen how Jesus touches our dirt—gets into our sicknesses, our illnesses—He touches us—then *we walk it out*.

We have to take the truth Jesus gives us and line up our steps in obedience to Him. Even after He's set us free from the dirt, we still have to *choose* to let it go. Jesus has given us the freedom to put it behind us—forever. Once we have been "washed" off, we can be the multiplied miracle God has called us to be.

> *...Put off, concerning your former conduct, the old man which grows corrupt according to the deceitful lusts, and be renewed in the spirit of your mind, and that you put on the new man which was created according to God,...* (Ephesians 4:22-24).

We are putting off the old man and putting on the new man. We are putting off anger, rage, malice, bitterness, unforgiveness. Through these steps that God has given us, we are putting on the new man: love, a sound mind, sound reasoning, a whole heart. We are exchanging the dirt, the garbage...and getting the divine. We say, "You can have that mud!" and we're receiving the miracle from Him.

> *To give them beauty for ashes, the oil of joy for mourning, the garment of praise for the spirit of heaviness; that they may be called trees of righteousness, the planting of the Lord, that He may be glorified* (Isaiah 61:3).

We are making a divine exchange: we give Him our ashes—He gives us His beauty. We give Him our sorrow, depression—He gives us His oil of joy.

Healed Inside and Out

Now we come to the most important part of this whole story—the happy ending:

> *Jesus heard that they had cast him*

out; and when He had found him, He said to him, "Do you believe in the Son of God?"He answered and said, "Who is He,...Then he said, "Lord, I believe!" And he worshipped Him. And Jesus said, "For judgment I have come into this world, that those who do not see may see, and that those who see may be born blind." (John 9:35,36,38,39).

This man—who was healed of blindness, who became the multiplied miracle for his community—came back into contact with the author of his miracle. The Bible said that Jesus found him, and He asked him, "What's wrong?"

The man said, "Well, I'm getting harassed."

Jesus asked, "Do you believe in Me?"

The man said, "Lord, I believe." The man had received his physical healing, but in that moment when he acknowledged Jesus as his Lord, he received his spiritual healing.

By design, we were made to be hungry for our Creator. There's a gap, there's a missing part in our lives if Jesus is not our Lord. That man could have walked away with a physical healing...and still missed his heart healing, his eternity in Christ. But Jesus came back and found him, and said, "It's not enough that you got a physical healing, now I want to give you a heart healing. I want to bring you back into original relationship with Me."

We were made to be hungry for our Creator.

All of us have dirt in our lives, but we don't have to stay in it. We can take these steps to turn our dirt into mud and have that mud turn into a miracle. We can't help but be grateful to the One Who isn't afraid to touch our dirt, to get into our innermost lives, to turn us into perfection, the way He always intended for us to be. We desire to be multiplied miracles, to share His wonderful works with our communities, with our leaders, with our families. And most of all, we want Him to have access to our hearts—to heal us inside and out.

PART FOUR

Living on the Edge

- **Chapter 12**
  Last Straws, Frazzled Ends, and Ragged Edges
- **Chapter 13**
  Desperate Edges
- **Chapter 14**
  Taking Advantage of Life's Edges
- **Chapter 15**
  The Winner's Edge: Grasp Your Success

Chapter 12

Last Straws, Frazzled Ends, and Ragged Edges

This world is going at a fast pace. We push to go faster and farther, with more efficiency, but many of us feel like we just barely make it from day to day. We do the best we possibly can—but it seems like we're constantly just squeaking by. We're not quite going over the edge, but we're certainly living on the edge.

Some of us also feel like we've reached the limits of our patience, "This is the last straw! I can't handle any more. If I don't have a miracle, I'm going to go totally over the edge and have a nervous breakdown."

In the last part of this book, we're going to learn how to find new strength to carry that "last straw"...how to handle the frazzled ends with success...how to turn defeat into victory...and how to live successfully and fearlessly on the edge. Now is the time to do more than just barely get by or be defeated by those edges in the frazzled world! This is the time to have victory, obtain success, move in miracles, and to see God's goodness manifested in our lives!

Edges can have two effects: injury or benefit. Ice skates are great examples of "edges." Ice skates have blades that need to be very sharp or dullness will affect skating ability and slow the skater down or cause him to fall. And if the skater is not careful when he falls, he can can be injured, even seriously hurt. The same is true for us in our lives: if we're not careful with the edges in our lives, they can defeat us, hurt us, and damage us permanently. That's not God's plan.

An edge can also be beneficial. Look at the same example with the ice skates. A friend of ours came over with his little 3-year old son, Rudy. Rudy was just like his father, really into hockey. Rudy started pretending he was ice-skating on our kitchen floor and his Dad said, "Rudy, Rudy, use the edges, use the edges!"

I thought, "What does that mean?" But then it started to sink into my brain. The skater will push off on the edges to get speed. If the edges are sharp, the skater will have greater maneuvering ability. Edges can hurt...or they can be beneficial.

The Edge That Hurts

The first unsuccessful edge we're going to look at is "the edge that hurts." We come up to the edge and we're at the limit, the very last straw. We just can't make it any farther. We say, "That's it, I've had it! I'm at the very end of my rope!" This edge can either be a benefit and blessing, or it can totally defeat us. This is the edge the Israelites found themselves on after spying out the Promised Land:

And they gave the children of Israel a bad report of the land which they had spied out, saying, "The land through which we have gone as spies is a land that devours its inhabitants, and all the people whom we saw in it are men of great stature. There we saw the giants (the descendants of Anak came from the giants); and we were like grasshoppers in our own sight, and so we were in their sight" (Numbers 13:32,33).

So all the congregation lifted up their voices and cried, and the people wept that night. And all the children of Israel complained against Moses and Aaron, and the whole congregation said to them, "If only we had died in the land of Egypt! Or if only we had died in this wilderness!" (Numbers 14:1,2).

The Israelites were at Kadesh, the

southern border of the Promised Land, and were about to enter. They were *right* at the edge. Twelve spies had gone out, checked everything, and come back with their reports. This was the last straw for the Israelites; this was their edge.

How did they behave at their edge? What did they say? Ten of the twelve spies said, "We cannot take the land." Then the people began to gripe and complain (one thing they were very good at doing!). They said, "We should have stayed in Egypt." They were slaves in Egypt! Now they were at their border, their edge, just about ready to attain their Promised Land...and they complained.

Teetering on the Edge

Their leaders, Moses and Aaron, and two of the twelve spies, Joshua and Caleb, tried to encourage them and reason with them:

> *...The land we passed through to spy out is an exceedingly good*

> *land. If the LORD delights in us, then He will bring us into this land and give it to us, a land which flows with milk and honey. Only do not rebel against the LORD, nor fear the people of the land, for they are our bread; their protection has departed from them, and the LORD is with us. Do not fear them* (Numbers 14:7-9).

They were almost there, but the Israelites complained, "Oh, this is terrible. God's promises will never come true!" And that's exactly what happened. That bad attitude on the edge defeated them. What do we do when we're at our last straw? What do we do at the end of our rope? What do we do when we're living on a ragged edge? Be careful how you speak!

> *Then the LORD said to Moses, "How long will these people reject Me? And how long will they not believe Me,*

> *with all the signs which I have performed among them?...They certainly shall not see the land of which I swore to their fathers, nor shall any of those who rejected Me see it"* (Numbers 14:11,23).

It is important what we do when we're at our edge because it determines whether we get a miracle or defeat.

Return to Kadesh

> *Then the children of Israel, the whole congregation, came into the Wilderness of Zin in the first month, and the people stayed in Kadesh; and Miriam died there and was buried there. Now there was no water for the congregation; so they gathered together against Moses and Aaron* (Numbers 20:1,2).

Here the people of Israel came to Kadesh *again*. They kept coming right to the edge of the Promised Land again and again—living their lives on the same edge over and over again. They came back to this place a total of thirty-two times!

In this situation, the Israelites didn't have any water. In classic Israelite style, they complained! "Oh, we don't have any water. We should have stayed back in Egypt!" They were at the edge of their Promised Land, and that edge had defeated them before. They had complained before. This time, they're at the same edge...and what did they do? They complained again! What were the results of their complaining? They brought more trouble on themselves and even on Moses!

> *Then the LORD spoke to Moses, saying, "Take the rod; you and your brother Aaron gather the congregation together. Speak to the rock before their eyes, and it will yield its water; thus you shall bring water for them out of the rock, and*

> *give drink to the congregation and their animals...." Then Moses lifted his hand and struck the rock twice with his rod; and water came out abundantly....Then the LORD spoke to Moses and Aaron, "Because you did not believe Me, to hallow Me in the eyes of the children of Israel, therefore you shall not bring this assembly into the land which I have given them"* (Numbers 20:7,8,11-13).

Moses was at the edge, "I've had it with these people. They frustrate me. They never do what I tell them to do. Look at them! They gripe, gripe, gripe! I'm fed up to here with all this stuff!"

God told Moses, "I want you to speak to the rock." He gave him explicit instructions how to bring about a miracle for the people. But Moses allowed his frustration to overwhelm him. He took his staff and he hit the rock instead of speaking to it.

Maybe Moses was even over the edge! He took out his frustration on the rock. He disobeyed and look what happened to him—there was no Promised Land for Moses or Aaron. The Lord said to Moses, "Because you did not trust Me enough to honor Me as holy in the sight of My people, you will not bring this community into the land that I am giving to them."

God wants to launch us into our next miracle!

Moses was at the end of his rope, he disobeyed, and the edge defeated him. It wasn't total defeat, because He did get water from the rock—but it could have been total victory. Ultimately, Moses was defeated at the edge, and he didn't get into the Promised Land.

When we are at our edge, how do we behave? It's not God's plan for the edge to defeat us or fill us full of fear. It's God's plan to launch us into our next miracle.

Back at the Edge Again!

Finally, the people of Israel came to Kadesh yet again, and this time, they wanted to keep on going:

> *Now Moses sent messengers from Kadesh to the king of Edom. "Thus says your brother Israel: 'You know all the hardship that has befallen us....When we cried out to the LORD, He heard our voice and sent the Angel and brought us up out of Egypt; Now here we are in Kadesh, a city on the edge of your border. Please let us pass through your country....' Then* [Edom] *said, "You shall not pass through." So Edom came out against them with many men and with a strong hand* (Numbers 20:14,16,17,20).

The Israelites were once again at Kadesh, and they wanted to travel through Edom. Now, remember, the people of

Edom were distant relatives of the Israelites. Moses addressed the king of Edom as "your brother Israel." There was a family precedent there.

They appealed to the king of Edom, "Hey, we just want to cut through on the King's highway here. If you give us permission, we'll pay you back. If we take anything, if there is any water missing or whatever, we'll make everything right. Just let us pass through." But the king of Edom refused.

Something happens when we come to that same edge repeatedly—our behavior changes. When we are continually defeated, we start to look for "human" ways to figure out how to bypass the problem. God never told the Israelites to bargain with the inhabitants of the Promised Land—He told them to defeat them! He didn't want His people making deals with the enemy.

Some of us keep coming back to the same place, the same edge, again and again. Like the children of Israel perched on the edge of the Promised Land, we stand at the edge of the situation that has always defeated us and sigh, "If only I could do it." It's time to wake up to the truth—it's *your* choice, but it's God's power that will take you through to success!

It is God's power that will take you through to success!

Your edge can be a constant negative in your life or it can become a place of great victory. Has a certain "edge" situation been a place of *continual* struggle or defeat for you? To break through to victory, change your choices! Are you tempted to complain about your situation or disobey God's precepts? Don't! Both are common temptation traps. Refuse to be ensnared by the very behavior that keeps you living in defeat.

Don't compromise! Do it God's way! Pray and confess, ask the Holy

Spirit for power, "I don't want to repeat the same self-defeating behavior. Will you show me how to avoid going through this edge situation again? Give me success—quickly! Thank you, God, for taking me through to a miracle victory!"

Chapter 13
Desperate Edges

In II Kings chapter 6, we read about another example of people living on the edge. This one was a total disaster. Samaria was under siege and in the middle of a famine. If we think *our* lives are tough, that *we're* living on the edge—wait until we see what *these* people went through!

> *And there was a great famine in Samaria; and indeed they besieged it until a donkey's head was sold for eighty shekels of silver, and one-fourth of a kab of dove droppings for five shekels of silver* (II Kings 6:25).

The people were so desperately on the edge that they were eating ugly, bony old donkey heads and dove droppings. They had no food, they were under siege by an enemy army. They were definitely on the edge!

> *Then, as the king of Israel was passing by on a wall, a woman cried out to him, saying, "Help, my LORD, O king!" And he said, "If the LORD does not help you, where can I find help for you? From the threshing floor or from the wine press?"* (II Kings 6:26,27).

Was the king at the edge? Absolutely! He said, "I can't help you if God can't help you."

> *Then the king said to her, "What is troubling you?" And she answered, "This woman said to me, 'Give your son, that we may eat him today, and we will eat my son tomorrow.' So we boiled my son, and ate him. And I said to her on the next day, 'Give your son, that we may eat him;' but she has hidden her son"* (II Kings 6:28,29).

Now the situation had turned gory and insane. The people became cannibals! This was an edge that's almost unimaginable. One desperate woman had persuaded this other woman to kill and cook her own son, promising that she would do the same thing with her son the next day. That was crazy, over the edge!

These were women beyond the verge of a nervous breakdown! Human behavior can become hideous at the edge. Then the woman had the audacity to complain to the king that her fellow cannibal wasn't keeping her word, but had hidden her son. Sometimes over-the-edge parents can do really nasty, cruel, inhuman things to their children.

I grew up with a friend who loved basketball, and was great at it. Her dad loved basketball, too, and he tried to live his life through her. When he got to his own edge in playing basketball, he never quite made it. So, he imposed his life on her. It was hard, and she wound up resenting and totally despising basketball.

When we get to our edge, if we're not careful, we'll look to the wrong things to resolve our problem.

Don't Just Sit There

> *Now there were four leprous men at the entrance of the gate; and they said to one another, "Why are we sitting here until we die? If we say, 'We will enter the city,' the famine is in the city, and we shall die there. And if we sit here, we die also. Now therefore, come, let us surrender to the army of the Syrians. If they keep us alive, we shall live; and if they kill us, we shall but die"* (II Kings 7:3,4).

Here was another group of people in the same situation, in the same famine, under the same siege. They were lepers, and they were at the edge. They weren't even in the city, but outside the gates.

> *And they rose at twilight to go to the camp of the Syrians; and when they had come to the outskirts of the Syrian camp, to their surprise no one was there* (II Kings 7:5).

What did these lepers do at their edge? They got up and moved. They behaved differently at the edge and God used them! These men approached the edge of the camp of the Syrians. Often, it's at the very edge of our desperate situation, that God totally turns the thing around.

> *For the LORD had caused the army of the Syrians to hear...the noise of a great army; so they said to one another, "Look, the king of Israel has hired against us the kings of the Hittites and the kings of the Egyptians to attack us!" Therefore they arose and fled at twilight, and left the camp intact—their tents, their horses, and their donkeys—*

> *and they fled for their lives. And when these lepers came to the outskirts of the camp, they...carried from it silver and gold and clothing....Then they said to one another, "...This day is a day of good news....Come, let us go and tell the king's household"* (II Kings 7:6-9).

Some people let their edge turn into hideous insanity. These lepers let their edge turn into a miracle that saved everyone!

When we reach our edge, it doesn't just affect us—it affects others as well. Our edge can be the turning point for someone else's victory miracle...or our edge can become hideous defeat affecting those around us. Sometimes we just get tunnel vision and ignore others, "*I'm* living on the edge. *I* can't handle it any more. *I'm* at the last straw." But our edge isn't meant to defeat or crush us—it's meant to push us into a greater miracle focus.

Mishandling the Edge

Remember the king of Samaria? He had been accosted by the woman who had eaten her own son. In his revulsion, in his anguish and unbelief, he threatened Elisha, the man of God:

> *...When the king heard the words of the woman,...he tore his clothes....Then he said, "God do so to me and more also, if the head of Elisha...remains on him today." ...And the king sent a man ahead of him, but before the messenger came to him,* [Elisha] *said to the elders, "Do you see how this son of a murderer has sent someone to take away my head?...Is not the sound of his master's feet behind him?" And while he was still talking...there was the messenger* (II Kings 6:30-33).

Then Elisha said, "Hear the word of

> *the LORD....'Tomorrow about this time a seah of fine flour shall be sold for a shekel, and two seahs of barley for a shekel, at the gate of Samaria.'" So an officer on whose hand the king leaned answered the man of God and said, "Look, if the LORD would make windows in heaven, could this thing be?" And he said, "In fact, you shall see it with your eyes, but you shall not eat of it"* (II Kings 7:1,2).

> *...So a seah of fine flour was sold for a shekel, and two seahs of barley for a shekel, according to the word of the LORD. Now the king had appointed the officer...to have charge of the gate. But the people trampled him in the gate, and he died, just as the man of God had said...* (II Kings 7:16,17).

The king sent his "right hand man," his most trusted advisor, to kill Elisha. Elisha said to him, "This situation is going to turn around tomorrow. Good things are going to happen. We're going to see a night-and-day change." But the king's advisor scoffed at Elisha's words.

So Elisha prophesied that this officer wouldn't see God's miracle. He said, "You are at the edge, and you don't believe. Therefore your edge is going to crush you." And the king's advisor died. We have to be careful what we believe and say at our edge.

Common Edge Errors

There are three common errors that occur when we're living on the edge. These mistakes cause the edge to overwhelm us and bring us into defeat.

• Number One: Complaints

How did the Israelites behave when they came to Kadesh, when they came to the edge that defeated them? They complained! "This is the pits! We might as well just throw in the towel." That's not smart "edge behavior."

• Number Two: Disobedience

Another common edge error is disobedience. We hear something that we know is the right thing to do, but we don't do it. Moses struck the rock instead of speaking to it, as God had clearly instructed him. That's disobedience—and it cost him a very high price. We know the right thing to do inside, but when we get to the very edge of something, we say, "Ah, just forget it." We go off and disobey.

Our actions on the edge determine whether we will have victory.

At edge turning-point times, it's critical to be careful what we do, what we think, how we behave, how we approach that edge. Our actions on the edge will determine whether we will be crushed or whether we will have victory.

• Number Three: Unbelief

A third common edge error is unbelief.

A lady was talking to me about her son who had just graduated from college. She was really having a hard time with him because he had absolutely no interest in God. He was rude to her and she was trying to say, "You need God! You don't know how much you need God. Now you need Him more than ever since you're out of college and on the edge of the real world." She was at the edge with her son, but he was in unbelief and refusing to go to the edge with God.

At the edge, what do we believe? Do we believe the edge is stronger than God, or is God stronger than the edge? Unbelief is a common edge error because the impossible thing that has happened seems to be so horrific and so huge that it can overwhelm us.

We cannot make the edge bigger than God. God is bigger than our edge. God wants to meet us at our edge, and help us get over the edge into a miracle!

Chapter 14
Taking Advantage of Life's Edges

We have seen how the edges can try and defeat us. Now we're going to look at how we can use the edge for our advantage.

Let's look at I Kings chapter 17:

> *Then the word of the LORD came to* [Elijah], *saying, "...Go to Zarephath, ...I have commanded a widow there to provide for you." ...When he came to the gate of the city, indeed a widow was there ....He called to her and said, "Please bring me a little water in a cup, that I may drink." And as she was going to get it, he called to her and said, "Please bring me a morsel of bread in your hand." So she said, "...I do not have bread, only a handful of flour...and a little*

> *oil...and see, I am gathering a couple of sticks that I may go in and prepare it for myself and my son, that we may eat it, and die."*
>
> *...Elijah said to her, "Do not fear;...do as you have said, but make me a small cake...first...and afterward make some for yourself and your son. For thus says the LORD God of Israel: 'The...flour shall not be used up, nor shall the...oil run dry, until the day the Lord sends rain on the earth." So she...did according to the word of Elijah.... The...flour was not used up, nor did the jar of oil run dry...* (I Kings 17:8-16).

God told Elijah to go into a certain town where a widow would meet him and feed him. Elijah obediently got up and went to the edge of the city, where he found this woman. He said to her, "Please give me something to drink"—so she gave him something to drink. Then he added,

"And please give me something to eat."

What did she say? She was at the very edge of her supply. She said, "Well, I was collecting sticks so that I could cook the last amount of bread I have. My son and I would have our last meal and then die." She was totally at the edge! But what happened?

Elijah said to her, "Go ahead, cook it...but give it to me instead—and as you give it to me, you'll see that the supply won't run out until it starts to rain!" And that is exactly what happened. She obeyed at her edge. Had she not given her food to him, the edge would have consumed her and she would have died. She was obedient...and the edge became a miracle!

Faith-Building Edges

In the natural, the widow estimated that there was enough flour and oil to make one small cake. She could have calculated: "Let's see, one cake divided by two for my son and me—that's half a piece of cake each. Or, I bake the cake and divide it by three for this visiting prophet here and my son and me—that's a third of a piece of cake each. Oh dear, what shall I do?"

She couldn't see what the man of God could see: an unlimited supply of flour and oil—enough to feed him, herself, her son, and her entire household, until the end of the drought! But she didn't need to see what the prophet could see—she simply needed to obey. Her faith kicked in, and she got her miracle at the edge!

What did this miracle do to this widow's faith? It totally built her faith, so much so that when her son died, she had faith that God could raise him from the dead. (See I Kings 17:17-24.)

Our edges aren't meant to defeat us; they're meant to give us more faith! They are meant to build our faith, so that at the next challenge we have stronger faith to match and overcome it. We don't have to be defeated at the edge and have

"Kadesh" defeats. We must search for the "widow and Elijah" experiences! We will be rewarded with abundant supply and miraculous provision totally beyond our abilities. Does that build our confidence and trust in God? Massively!

Another Faith-Building Edge

Let's look back one more time at the Israelites. Notice these aren't the same Israelites from Numbers chapter 13. The "Kadesh Israelites" who complained and wandered in the desert for forty years—had all died off. This is a new generation of Israelites. What happened at this edge is very important:

> *Then Joshua rose early in the morning; and they set out from Acacia Grove and came to the Jordan, he and all the children of Israel, and lodged there before they*

> *crossed over. So it was, after three days, that the officers went through the camp; and they commanded the people, saying, "When you see the ark of the covenant of the LORD your God, and the priests, the Levites, bearing it, then you shall set out from your place and go after it"* (Joshua 3:1-3).

They weren't in the Promised Land yet. They had come to the Jordan River, and they camped there for three days. Later in the chapter, it tells us that the Jordan River was at flood stage. (See Joshua 3:15,16.) The Jordan was not just a little trickling canal—it was a flooding river that ran very high.

Sometimes at our edge, it seems like we're there for an eternity. "I'm waiting! Hello? I'm on the edge. There is the river, there is the other side...and I'm waiting!" They were there for three days, and what were they doing? Nothing. They were patiently waiting.

Sometimes the edge defeats us because we get impatient. "Come on! Don't You know I'm on a time-line, God?" Of course He knows that—but we're not on His time line. We have to adjust and get on His time line.

We have to get on God's time line.

These patient Israelites waited for three days, then the officers went through the camp giving orders. (See Joshua 3:2-4.) "When you see the Ark of the Lord, get yourselves together. We're going to cross the Jordan!"

All of the Israelites were watching the leadership. Nobody was building pontoons to cross over. Nobody was working on a bridge to cross over. Nobody was breaking out the rubber rafts and loading them up in order to cross over.

Nobody seemed to be doing anything (in the natural) to get across that river. Yet they were supposed to collect themselves because they were going to cross. There seemed no possible way to cross the river. These Israelites were at the edge of their impossibility.

A Miracle at the Edge

Joshua was their leader, and he had two million people with him. He was at the edge, "Come on, God. This would be a really good, really convenient time for a miracle right now."

> *And the Lord said to Joshua, "This day I will begin to exalt you in the sight of all Israel, that they may know that, as I was with Moses, so I will be with you. You shall command the priests who bear the ark of the covenant, saying, 'When you have come to the edge of the water of the Jordan, you shall stand in the Jordan'"* (Joshua 3:7,8).

God said to Joshua, "Tell the priests

who carry the Ark of the Covenant, when they reach the edge of the Jordan's water to go and stand in the river."

"Wonderful! We're going to wade over, or carry each other over! All the time, we'll have this heavy Ark of the Covenant to carry too. Come on, give me a break!" But is that what happened?

> *So it was, when the people set out ...to cross over the Jordan, with the priests bearing the ark of the covenant...and the feet of the priests who bore the ark dipped in the edge of the water...that the waters...from upstream stood still, and rose in a heap very far away....So the waters that went down into...the Salt Sea, failed, and were cut off; and the people crossed over opposite Jericho. Then the priests who bore the ark of the covenant of the Lord stood firm on dry ground in the midst of the Jordan; and all Israel crossed over on dry ground, until all the*

> *people had crossed completely over the Jordan* (Joshua 3:14-17).

Sometimes it seems that we come to the edge, just hanging over the edge, and we cry, "God, help me!" That's when God says, "I'm here, and I've got your miracle!" Never discount God's ability to come through at the edge! The Israelites couldn't afford to doubt Him, and neither can we. They got their extraordinary miracle! Meet God at the edge, and He will meet you.

Chapter 15
The Winner's Edge: Grasp Your Success

Finally, let's look at Gideon and his edge. He didn't have much courage in the beginning. When we first meet Gideon, he was trying to hide the wheat harvest from the Midianites, and the Angel of the Lord came directly to him and picked him out:

> *Now the Angel of the LORD came and sat under the terebinth tree which was in Ophrah...while... Gideon threshed wheat in the winepress, in order to hide it from the Midianites. And the Angel of the LORD appeared to him, and said to him, "The LORD is with you, you mighty man of valor!"*

Gideon said to Him, "O my LORD, if the LORD is with us, why then has all this happened to us? ...The LORD has forsaken us and delivered us into the hands of the Midianites."

Then the LORD turned to him and said, "Go in this might of yours, and you shall save Israel from the hand of the Midianites. Have I not sent you?" So he said to Him, "O my LORD, how can I save Israel?"...And the LORD said to him, "Surely I will be with you, and you shall defeat the Midianites as one man" (Judges 6:11-16).

That conversation has so much irony and humor in it! I can just hear Gideon, offering excuses and wimping out...and the Angel of the Lord just chuckling and encouraging him to see past his own limitations. Gideon went on to make sacrifices to the Lord, but even in his timidity he tried to downplay his own ability:

> *So Gideon took ten men from among his servants and did as the LORD had said to him. But because he feared his father's household and the men of the city too much to do it by day, he did it by night* (Judges 6:27).

Gideon was a classic case of a guy stuck on the edge—paralyzed by his own shortcomings and afraid of men. He was trying everything except God's way to survive. So why did God select him from among the people? Because He knew that He could use Gideon to get the job done!

> *And He said to me, "My grace is sufficient for you, for My strength is made perfect in weakness..."* (II Corinthians 12:9).

Gideon didn't have much tolerance for stress. Some people can tolerate a whole lot of stress and trauma, and others can't. Gideon was one of those who couldn't take trauma. He needed God's kind of strength and courage to succeed.

God's Plan on the Edge

The Midianite army was massive. There were so many of them that the Bible says they looked like locusts—destroying everything in their path. They numbered as many as the sands on the seashore. (See Judges 6:5;7:12.) We have to remember that Gideon thought he was a *nobody* from *nowhere*, but because the hand of the Lord was upon him, 32,000 people decided to follow him and fight against the Midianites.

> *And the Lord said to Gideon, "The people who are with you are too many for Me to give the Midianites into their hands, lest Israel claim glory for itself against Me, saying, 'My own hand has saved me'...by the three hundred men who lapped I will save you, and deliver the*

Midianites into your hand..." (Judges 7:2,7).

So God started weeding his army down—from 32,000 to 10,000, then from 10,000 down to 300. (See Judges 7:3-7.) God was ready to pitch three hundred men against countless Midianites. Now that created quite an interesting edge for Gideon, didn't it?

Gideon said, "Give me a break! Three hundred against that huge army?" The Bible said he was afraid:

...The LORD said to him, "...Go down to the camp with Purah your servant, and you shall hear what they say; and afterward your hands shall be strengthened to go down against the camp..." (Judges 7:9-11).

God strengthened Gideon and helped him work through his fear. He told Gideon to sneak over to the Midianite camp and listen to what they were saying about him. So Gideon went down to the edge of the Midianite camp, and it was at that edge that he got his encouragement:

> *And when Gideon had come, there was a man telling a dream to his companion. He said, "I have had a dream: to my surprise, a loaf of barley bread tumbled into the camp of Midian; it came to a tent and struck it so that it fell and overturned, and the tent collapsed."*
>
> *Then his companion answered and said, "This is...but the sword of Gideon the son of Joash, a man of Israel! Into his hand God has delivered Midian and the whole camp."...Gideon ...returned to the camp of Israel, and said, "Arise, for the LORD has delivered the camp of Midian into your hand!"* (Judges 7:13-15).

Can you just imagine what was going through Gideon's mind as he heard that conversation? "How in the world have these two strangers, these Midianites even heard of me? I'm nobody special. It really must be the Lord God speaking to them through their dreams! The only way they could even know about me—even my whole name!—is because God spoke to them. And since this is what He said—that the whole camp is going to be delivered into my hands—then it must be true!" Often it's at the edge that, if we're listening to God carefully, we'll get our encouragement.

Believing at the Edge

So Gideon got his encouragement on the edge, but now he had to communicate that to his three hundred remaining men:

> *Then...he put a trumpet into every man's hand, with empty pitchers; and torches inside the pitchers. And he said to them, "Look at me and do likewise; watch, and when I come to*

> *the edge of the camp you shall do as I do. When I blow the trumpet...then you also blow the trumpets on every side of the whole camp, and say, 'The sword of the LORD and of Gideon!'"*
>
> *So Gideon and the hundred men who were with him came to the outpost of the camp...they blew the trumpets and broke the pitchers that were in their hands....And they cried, "The sword of the LORD and of Gideon!" And...the whole army ran and cried out and fled* (Judges 7:16-21).

Gideon told his men, "Watch me, and follow my lead. When I get to the edge of the camp, do exactly what I do." Picture this: Gideon had three hundred men, which he divided up into smaller groups, and the Midianites had this massive, sands-of-the-sea-sized army. How could the Midianites believe that Gideon and the boys were going to conquer them? But they followed and were obedient to God, right to the edge of the camp.

Did those three hundred men with Gideon say, "This guy has lost it! He's insane?" They had come to the edge of the camp where there was no turning back at the edge. Did they say, "Oops, I'm sorry! I can't handle this. See you later!"? No way! They had committed themselves ...and the edge of the camp was where they would find their miracle.

This tiny army blew their trumpets and broke their jars making a horrendous noise. The whole Midianite army thought there was a massive number of people surrounding them, and they ran away. Gideon and the boys got to the edge...and their edge became the Midianites' downfall!

How about our edge? How about our impossible situation? How about when you're at the end of your rope? In God, there is no end of the rope. God's rope is endless; it keeps going and going. God has miracle rope and He can make the rope longer for us.

Gideon had a total miracle on the edge. He didn't even have traditional weapons with which to fight. He used trumpets and broken lamps to defeat his enemy. Our edges are not meant to defeat us. God gives us edges to enhance and to sharpen our victories. He intends for the edge times to improve us, to sharpen us and to make us more successful. Edges are meant to elevate us to a higher level in God.

Edge Success for You

In a previous chapter, we looked at some common edge *errors*, things to avoid. We should avoid complaining at our edge, we need to watch out for unbelief, we need to avoid disobedience. Now let's review some common components of edge *success*—things we should do when we're at our edge.

Stretch out! Go a little further. Maybe this is your sixth time around Jericho and it's only one more day until you get your victory. Think of it: if the Israelites had awakened on the seventh day of marching around Jericho and said, "This is pretty bland and boring here. We've done the same thing for the last six days, and we don't see even a single rock moving in that wall. Let's just forget this and call it a bad attempt." It was on their seventh day that they got their victory! Stretch out!

How about the leprous men? They didn't sit back at the city gate and say, "Oh well, we're just going to have to be defeated by this famine. It's bad enough that we are lepers, but we're going to starve too." No. They stretched out. I encourage you: stretch out at your edge.

Be Obedient

Look at the starving widow. She was obedient, even when it seemed totally unreasonable. She was facing starvation. And it seemed so absurd and foolish to give her last little bit of food away, but she was obedient, and she received her miracle.

How about our edge? We need to be obedient to the things God tells us to do. Some of us are at our edge with our finances—are we tithing? Be obedient! A lot of times, it's at our edge that we're going to have the turn around for our miracle.

Watch the Source

Often we'll come up to the edge of our "Jordan River" and it will be flooded and seem completely impossible to cross. We get our focus too much on the problem, "This will never happen. I'm just going to throw in the towel. Forget it. Look at this river! It's huge! I'll never get across." If we look at the impossibility, the edge will overwhelm us. We must keep our focus on God.

Look at the people with Gideon. Gideon said, "Follow my lead." Whose lead are we following at our edge? If we're following Jesus' lead, the edge won't crush us. If we're looking to Jesus, we'll have success and prosperity. We'll come out better than when we started—at the edge.

But if we follow our own lead or the defeating lead, we'll just hit a dead end.

Patience

Be patient at the edge. Often we get on this time schedule—"Come on, get with it! Can't you see I need this now?"—but we need to be patient. The Israelites at the Jordan waited three days. How about us? Sometimes it's hard for us to be patient at our edge, but we need to be. We need patience because the victory at the outcome of our edge will be worth our patience.

> *My brethren, count it all joy when you fall into various trials, knowing that the testing of your faith produces patience. But let patience have its perfect work, that you may be perfect and complete, lacking nothing* (James 1:2-4).

When we're patient, God does some absolutely wonderful things in our lives.

AFTERWORD

Years ago, I was at a restaurant with my mother, just sitting there eating chips and dip, and I told her, "I don't believe that Jesus is the Son of God." Can you imagine how that must have shocked her? The daughter of Marilyn Hickey is doubting *the most basic* Christian belief—the deity of Christ? I had taken my mother to the edge and I anticipated dire consequences.

Mom surprised me. I expected her to be very upset, perhaps cut off my college funds, or even disown me. I was ready to argue my position with what I thought was clear, inescapable logic. However, none of that happened—there was no scene, no debate, and no hard feelings! No hurtful things were said and no barriers were erected between us.

Instead she showed understanding and love for me. She said, "Your father and I loved you before you believed in Jesus, when you were only a baby, and we will continue to love you no matter what you believe." She totally disarmed an explosive situation and paved my way to return from the edge.

How could she react that way? Why didn't she go through the roof? Her faith wasn't in her ability to argue me out of my silly beliefs, browbeat me into submitting to her authority, or manipulate me with finances into a fingers-crossed-behind-my-back agreement with her point of view. Mom's faith was in God's Word and His power to bring me back to the truth from a fatal error...and it worked. Thank God it worked! Eventually, the day came that I gave up my mistaken point of view and returned to a belief in Jesus as the Christ, the Son of God.

Everyone has a different reason for being on the edge, but the way back is the same for everyone—trust God. If you remember only one thing from this book, remember this: *God will* bring you back from the edge of destruction *if* you will put your faith in Him. I believe God is saying to you, right now...

> *...I am the LORD, your God, who takes hold of your right hand and says to you, Do not fear; I will help you* (Isaiah 41:13 NIV).

If you're hanging precariously from a crumbling ledge and there's nothing but ruin and destruction below—reach up...turn to God...trust Him with your situation...and He *will* take your hand and bring you to safety.

Receive Jesus Christ as Lord and Savior of Your Life.

The Bible says, *"That if thou shalt confess with thy mouth the Lord Jesus, and shalt believe in thine heart that God hath raised him from the dead, thou shalt be saved. For with the heart man believeth unto righteousness; and with the mouth confession is made unto salvation"* (Romans 10:9,10).

To receive Jesus Christ as Lord and Savior of your life, sincerely pray this prayer from your heart:

Dear Jesus,

I believe that You died for me and that You rose again on the third day. I confess to You that I am a sinner and that I need Your love and forgiveness. Come into my life, forgive my sins, and give me eternal life. I confess You now as my Lord. Thank You for my salvation!

Signed____________________ Date______________

Mr. & Mrs.
Mr.
Miss
Mrs.

Please print.

Name ____________________________________

Address __________________________________

City _______________ State/Province ________

Zip/Postal Code ___________________________

Country __________________________________

Phone (H) ( ) _________________________

Email ____________________________________

Contact us at: Marilyn Hickey Ministries • P.O. Box 17340 • Denver, CO 80217 • 1-303-770-0400 • **www.mhmin.org**

Prayer Request(s)

Let us join our faith with yours for your prayer needs. Fill out the coupon below and send to Marilyn Hickey Ministries, P.O. Box 17340, Denver, CO 80217.

Prayer Request(s) ______________________________

____

____

____

____

____

Please print.

Name Mr. & Mrs. / Mr. / Miss / Mrs. ______________________________

Address ______________________________

City ________________ State/Province __________

Zip/Postal Code ______________________________

Country ______________________________

Phone (H) (   ) ______________________________

Email ______________________________

If you need prayer, contact us: www.mhmin.org

For Your Information

❑ Please send me your **free monthly magazine,** OUTPOURING (including daily devotionals, timely articles, and ministry updates)!

❑ Please send me Marilyn and Sarah's **latest product catalog.**

❑ Check us out online at **www.mhmin.org**

Mr. & Mrs.
Mr.
Miss
Mrs.

Please print.

Name ______________________________

Address ______________________________

City ______________ State/Province ________

Zip/Postal Code ______________________________

Country ______________________________

Phone (H) ( ) ______________________________

Email ______________________________

Mail to:

Marilyn Hickey Ministries

P.O. Box 17340

Denver, CO 80217

1-303-770-0400

www.mhmin.org

Meet Sarah Bowling...

Sarah Bowling is the daughter of Pastor Wallace and Marilyn Hickey. Sarah has a God-given gift for teaching and ministry. Exhibiting a level of wisdom and maturity beyond her years, her energy and enthusiasm are appreciated by audiences of all ages.

Sarah's ministry focus is reaching the lost and teaching the Word with signs and wonders following. She travels and ministers worldwide in countries of the former Soviet Union, Africa, Pakistan, South America, the United Kingdom, France, and others. She has been a guest on TBN's PRAISE THE LORD! television programs and RICHARD ROBERTS LIVE! Sarah is a regular on the TODAY WITH MARILYN AND SARAH daily telecast, viewed in more than 350 million homes, worldwide.

Sarah, her husband, Reece, and their daughter, Isabell, live in Denver, Colorado, where they work with Marilyn Hickey Ministries and serve as associate pastors at Orchard Road Christian Center.

Through the Years With Sarah

Sarah traveled often as a child with parents Wallace and Marilyn Hickey to exotic lands such as Egypt, China, and Israel.

At an early age, God planted a love and gift for missions in Sarah's heart.

Sarah and her husband, Reece, joined the MHM staff in 1995. Sarah is also on staff at Word to the World College and maintains a busy home and ministry calling–traveling, teaching, and ministering worldwide.

Sarah has been on many short-term mission trips and has ministered in Russia, Africa, France, Pakistan, Australia, and the UK.

Wherever she teaches the Bible, Sarah brings a fresh update on what the Holy Spirit is doing around the world. Check out Sarah's page. www.mhmin.org